AFRIC

CW00545819

Our Global Destiny

By Archbishop Doyé Agama

Thursday 25·01·2018

An environmentally friendly book printed and bound in England by
www.printondemand-worldwide.com

http://www.fast-print.net/bookshop

AFRICA, CHRISTIANITY AND THE BIBLE
Copyright © Archbishop Doyé Agama 2016

Unless otherwise stated, all Scripture references are from the Holy Bible,
New King James Version (NKJV), Copyright © 1982 by Thomas Nelson, Inc.

A catalogue record for this book is available from the British Library

ISBN 978-178456-312-7

First published 2016 by
FASTPRINT PUBLISHING
Peterborough, England.

Introduction

This book will tell you the truth about African history from a biblical viewpoint as we investigate the relationship between Africa, Christianity and the Bible. To do this, we shall avoid the classical history mind-set of Europe. Christianity was not a European religion in its origins and we will see how the narrative of the Bible fits so neatly with the history of the great African continent, the Mother Land of Akebu, Aksum, Ethiopia, Nubia, Egypt…and so much more…

Until the true story of Africa is told, the history of the World is only half told, for from antiquity, Africa has been the source of vast riches of science, culture, minerals, agriculture, religion and of course, her people who have enhanced every civilisation of the world. Considering the vast nature of our subject, we will use two African Nations, Egypt and Nigeria for many of our examples.

By broadly following the story of Salvation for humanity in the Holy Bible, this book does two things. Firstly, it give us a structure or framework for our study of and understanding of Africa and secondly, it also removes the lie that Christianity and the Bible are foreign to Africa. In fact we shall find that not only Christianity, but Judaism, itself, have deep connections with the continent of Africa. We will also find that the blood line of Christ has been repeatedly preserved and nurtured by Africa and this we shall also see is a source of great tension and hatred between the enemies of Christ and Africa.

However those who seek to prove that everything good about the world came only from Africa and that everyone worthy of any note was a Black African will be disappointed. This book avoids the traps of ethnic or racial particularism and the Christocentric epistemology also avoids the Europeanisation of Jesus Christ. It places the Messiah firmly in the context of the people and the lands in which He lived, and their proximity to, and interactions with the real life of the continent of Africa.

At the same time, this book does not shy away from confronting the global strategic implications of the facts of African history. We shall also see something of the effects of climate change and the migrations out of and back into Africa, and how the sons and daughters of Africa took civilisation from the continent far beyond what the available history textbooks would ever dare to tell us.

While it is not an academic treatise, this book does hope to make a contribution to the conversation. The narrative in this book adopts a holistic hermeneutic that attempts to weave the geographical, cultural, historical and spiritual strands into a composite approach, which hopefully avoids the individualistic atomisation of classic European academic intellectualism and the consequent reactionary responses of afro-centric historians. This book places Africa and Africans firmly within the wider family of humanity and the broader narrative of world history, using the framework of the bible and its relationship to Africa. While much of the book will be the ancient stories of Africa, space will be given to more recent histories of Christianity in the struggles for independence, the Cold War and the rise of modern militant Islamic Jihad, which some may say has never really left the African continent.

It is important to state that this book has no intention of being "anti-Islam". Most of the scenarios in this book are written from previously published material already easily available in the public domain. The majority of Moslems around the world are generally peaceful people who just want to live their lives. Unfortunately, moderate Moslems have been shown to have no control over what the radical Islamists do. Moderate Moslems themselves are often the target and victims of the radicals.

Our subject is Africa, Christianity and the Bible; our Global Destiny. We shall review the influence of

Africa on the ancestry of Christ and the often critical role of Africa in fulfilling Bible prophecy. This we will see is the true spiritual reason for the subsequent suffering of Africa, and not the proverbial "Curse of Ham". We will mainly observe those in the lineage of Christ as it appears in the Gospel of Matthew, but we will also look at others mentioned in the Gospel of Luke. We are also studying some others in the Bible who are not directly in the lineage of Christ, but who had a significant connection with Africa or Africans. Finally we will look at those in the Renewed Testament of Christ who were affected by their relationship with the children of Ham. In the final section, we look at the role of Africans in the continuing story of Christianity and the destiny of Africa on the global stage.

Contents

Chapter One – The Original Africans

The term Africa originally refers to a people. They are the Afri. They are the tribe that was found in North Africa and the Afri people were probably related to the Berber people who stretched all across that North African coast. So, when others who sailed on the Mediterranean came and asked who they were, they said "we are the Afri", and the visitors began to call that land Africa and its people Africans. The name Afri belonged to a people, one of the indigenous peoples of North Africa. Perhaps we should remember that North Africa was not originally inhabited by Arabs. North Africa was inhabited by other indigenous African peoples long, long, long before the Islamic (and other) invasions.

Ethnically Africa today is one of the most diverse places on Earth. In fact many of the people that you think of today as Africans and even Sub Saharan Africans are relatively recent arrivals. In fact most people that you think of as Black Africans are more closely related genetically today, to what you think of as White Europeans than they are to some of the other black peoples, for example, the Australoid Negrito and other ethnic groupings in the Pacific such as the Andamanese, Semang, Mani, Aeta, Agta, Ati, and many others. The Nigritos for example are believed to have descended from a very early Great Migration out of Africa (Proto-Australoids) and are also distinct from the Asiatic people although they have intermarried with them. This migration and subsequent waves out of Africa are thought to have continued over land bridges (available due to lower ocean levels) and crossings of open seas, to produce the Australian Aborigines and other groups in Oceania. The historic African Migrations are thought to have continued eastward into China and also eventually westward, over the Bering Strait into North America and down into South America.

There have long been speculations about a large Black population in Ancient China, and that some of the early Chinese Emperors were in fact

Africans! These theories have claimed that Pu-yi of Manchukuo the last Emperor of China and the twelfth and final ruler of the Qing or Manchu Dynasty still showed the clear traces of this African Ancestry. DNA specialist, Jin Li headed a team of scientists who set out to show an independent origin of a unique strain of Chinese humanity, and announced DNA findings in 2005 that **proved** a common ancestry of 65 branches of the Chinese people that emerged from East Africa!

By contrast, several of those that we think of as Africans today, with an exception of a few in the southern tip of Africa (South Africa and Namibia for example) and in the east of Africa have moved in and out of Africa during their history. . An example of this is the Yoruba. The wider Yoruba speaking peoples are an ethnically diverse group, including some who were conquered by or otherwise assimilated into the ancient Yoruba empires and so historically they came to speak the same; or dialects of the same language. They do have oral traditions which claim they came back into Africa from somewhere in the Middle East, with connections to the Norther Kingdom of Israel, Saudi Arabia, or Baghdad, depending on which sources you read.

It is probably more likely though that while there were Yoruba indigenous to West Africa, certain royal Yoruba families were linked to the Middle East through later migrations and intermarriages between the arrivals and existing populations. A similar explanation may account for the tradition among the Kanuri of North East Nigeria that a son of Dhu Ifazan of Yemen named Sef, arrived in Kanem sometime before 900AD and became the link between the Kanuri and the Himyarite (Sayfawa) Dynasty of King Sayf ibn Dhī Yazan of Yemen, the king credited with ending Ethiopian (Aksumite) rule over Yemen and Southern Arabia. What is clear is that there have been movements of peoples into and out of the Sahara and wider Africa over many centuries, and some of those in the coastal regions of West Africa today may have memories of connections with people in what is today the Middle East.

A five-episode science documentary titled "The Incredible Human Journey" was first broadcast on BBC television in 2009 and sought to prove that the earliest European settlers were not White Caucasians, but dark skinned Africans! The TV series and the accompanying book were both, written and presented by Alice Roberts.

Africa and Ancient Greece

Greeks lived in Egypt and other parts of North Africa for almost a thousand years before the appearing of Christ in Bethlehem. There is no doubt that there was significant cultural economic and religious interaction between ancient Greece and ancient Africa including Egypt. Some historians have linked the Cretan and Minoan civilisations to African migration and/or colonisation. We will see below how the Libu of what became Cyrenaica intermarried with an early Greek migration.

Earliest contacts between Greece and Africa, were most likely to have been between Egypt and the Minoans of Bronze Age Crete. After a period of relative quiet, the interactions continued and flourished seven and eight hundred years before Christ. Black or dark skinned Africans (all known to Greeks as Ethiopians) are depicted in Greek art from both periods. Ethiopians were also depicted in tragedies and comedies ancient Greek drama. What is open to question is just how much interaction took place on the wider scale, and who influenced the other more; with supporters of opposing positions on this, each claiming victory.

What is probably indisputable is that ancient Greece had a high romantic view of Africa seeing its peoples as heroic and the hinterland of Africa as the holiday destination of some Greek Gods...

The Metropolitan Museum of Art in New York specialises in ancient Greece and Rome.

According to Sean Hemingway of the Department of Greek and Roman Art, of the museum and Colette Hemingway an Independent Scholar,

> *"Tales of Ethiopia as a mythical land at the farthest edges of the earth are recorded in some of the earliest Greek literature of the eighth century B.C., including the epic poems of Homer. Greek gods and heroes, like Menelaos, were believed to have visited this place on the fringes of the known world."(Hemmingway &Hemmingway, 2008)*

More mundanely, Africa was also important for Greek trade and North Africa was well know across the Mediterranean and beyond for supplies of grains, skins, and precious stones and metals from the interior of the continent.

The Libu of Cyrenaica

The Greek Colony of Cyrenaica (in today's Libya) contained many people of both European Greek and African ancestry, and many others of mixed heritage. The Libu and Tehenou were the original African tribes of the area that came to be called Cyrenaica. This area in Africa sometimes known as "Pentapolis", would play a repeated role in the story of Africa, Christianity and the Bible, and was home to Saint Mark the Apostle.

The Libu and the Tehenou who were probably related to the Afri and also to the Berber people of North Africa. They were allies with the Meshwesh, a Black African Kingdom just south of the Libu and Tehenou. The alliance of Libu-Meshwesh Kingdoms fought wars with Egypt 1300 years before Christ was born and ruled over Egypt for periods of time. Libu is the name from which the modern word Libya comes.

The first Greeks came to this part of Africa in the 7th Century BC from a Greek Island then called Thera (Santorini, in the southern Aegean Sea) to escape a desperate famine. The leaders of the Greek migration took on Libu (African) names and these Greeks lived amongst and intermarried with local African people. Other Greeks would join them later, but these original settlers (mixed Greek and Africans) remained the ruling class in Cyrene. These are the origins of the Cyrenians.

One Continent

The Bible account is that all the land on earth was originally one "super-continent" that was divided up later. We could suppose that any event on the scale of the great flood of scripture would have radically altered the Earth, but some features, including some of the very highest mountains survived and would still have served as landmarks. Noah and his family were the human survivors, and his sons and their descendants were Shem (Semitic – Middle Eastern), Ham (Hamitic – generally African, and Ethiopian also particularly referred to as Cushitic – Cush being the eldest son of Ham); and Japheth (Japhetic – Indo-European). Although these categories are no longer regarded as scientifically precise (and have suffered political and racially motivated use), they probably still shed important light on some ancient human history.

Named after Shem one of the sons of Noah (see below), Semitic is more of a linguistic than a precise ethnic classification. The term "sons" is generally used here in the sense of meaning "descendants". There are now some 700 million culturally and ethnically diverse speakers of nearly 80 branches of the Semitic languages, which are part of the wider Afro-Asiatic family of languages. Semitic languages are mostly found around the Middle East, but there are also huge populations of expatriate speakers of many of these languages around the world. The main Semitic groupings are Arabic, Amharic, Tigre and Tigrinya, and Hebrew. Also included are Ahlamu, Assyrian-Babylonian (Akkadian), Amharic, Amorite, Aramaic/Syriac, Canaanite (including Phoenician/Carthaginian), Chaldean, Eblaite, Edomite, Ge'ez, Maltese, Mandaic, Moabite, Sutean, Ugaritic, and many more... We shall see later that languages and cultures of people did change, or were affected by movements and migrations.

For example, the Sahara wasn't always a desert. Modern archaeology and space imaging proves that the Sahara was once largely arable and fertile enough to sustain large populations. There were movements of people into, and later out of what we now call the Sahara. There were at least three major river systems in the Sahara that coincide with ancient archaeological evidence of human settlement. Have you ever wondered, how come there are dried up river beds in the middle of a desert? What were they doing there? Before the Sahara became a desert, it once had settled communities, with domesticated agriculture both plant and animal, as well as sophisticated astronomy. Ancient Egypt owes much to these earlier civilisations, including the pyramid building kings of Nubia (Sudan), some of whom became influential Egyptian Pharaohs.

More than 30,000 Petroglyphs or rock engravings have been found in the Sahara. These drawings of animals on rocks are actually pictographs, a form of ancient African writing similar to the hieroglyphics of ancient Egypt. These were drawn in the Sahara by people who lived there, and had these animals around them there in what today is desert.

If the idea that humanity migrated out of Eden in Africa into Europe and other parts of the world is true, it needs to be taken with an assumption that the geography of the world then was probably very different. Interestingly, we still find the name ADEN very close to Africa. The Gulf of Aden and the Yemeni Port City of Aden are at the south western edge of the Arabian land mass, and sit just at the mouth of the East-African Rift Valley where the most ancient human remains have been found. As the name Rift Valley suggests, the separate pieces of land in this area were once closer together or a single land mass. If the Garden God planted east in Eden was at least partly in what is Africa today, does that make Adam and Eve the first Africans? Sometimes I wonder...

M. J. Benton, Barbara W. Murck and Brian J. Skinner argue that fossils of identical plants and animals have been found from South Africa to India to Australia and in West Africa and Brazil. The geology of parts of West Africa appears to match that of South America, as if they had once been joined. There is also the possibility that the Caledonian mountains of the British Isles, Scandinavia and Greenland are continued in the Appalachian Mountains, that extend up the Eastern United states of America and into Canada.

Ancient historians record a number of attempts (some successful) to link the Nile and the Red Sea. Several of these ancient canals were dug under the Pharaohs of Egypt. The modern Suez Canal was only completed in my lifetime. You may remember the troubles over the ownership and management of this canal, in which Great Britain got her political (and military) fingers badly burned.

And so in history you could walk from what is now Cape Town to Beijing China. It was possible, it was probably done. So these are the African people. Don't think of them as people who have always been in one place in Nigeria, in Ghana, in the Congo... There had been much movement over many centuries.

So these Hamitic, Cushitic Africans are the people who encompassed the areas that history knows as the cradles of civilisation. For if they inhabited the Tigris valley and if they also were in the Indus valley in India, if they also were in Egypt, then the early civilisations that we're talking about had much to do with the peoples that we describe as Africans.

Great movements of populations might have been possible in ancient times. Apart from the Nile, Niger, Benue, Congo, Orange, Limpopo and Zambesi, there were indeed other mighty rivers in Africa long ago. But as the Sahara dried some of its peoples were forced southward and began to encroach into the territory of others. Some of the coastal peoples of Africa could be the older peoples who were pushed down to the coast by more recent arrivals.

Starting from these basics, we get the beginnings of a different picture about who the peoples of Africa are. They are from their beginnings people who have adapted to circumstances who have survived great odds, who have covered great distances and achieved greatness in the midst of impossibilities, who have had to relocate to places and evolve new civilisations and make success from nothing. They are by their very nature from their history entrepreneurial people; people who refuse to be defeated; people who refuse to be destroyed. Africans can and will still rise again. Indeed both economic and political scientists are predicting that Africa will be the place of growth and prosperity in the future. In the next chapter, we look at the genealogy of Christ from the Gospel accounts of St Matthew and St Luke.

Chapter Two – The Bloodline (Genealogy) of Christ

St Matthew and St Luke each give us a similar lineage for Jesus Christ between Abraham and David. Both claim descent of Jesus Christ from King David, giving his a rightful claim to that ancient throne and the promise of God for an eternal kingdom. That promise is given in 2Samuel 7:8-17 and Jeremiah 33:17-21

> *2 Samuel 7:8-17 Now therefore, thus shall you say to My servant David, 'Thus says the Lord of hosts: "I took you from the sheepfold, from following the sheep, to be ruler over My people, over Israel. 9 And I have been with you wherever you have gone, and have cut off all your enemies from before you, and have made you a great name, like the name of the great men who are on the earth. 10 Moreover I will appoint a place for My people Israel, and*

will plant them, that they may dwell in a place of their own and move no more; nor shall the sons of wickedness oppress them anymore, as previously, 11 since the time that I commanded judges to be over My people Israel, and have caused you to rest from all your enemies. Also the Lord tells you that He will make you a house. 12 "When your days are fulfilled and you rest with your fathers, I will set up your seed after you, who will come from your body, and I will establish his kingdom. 13 He shall build a house for My name, and I will establish the throne of his kingdom forever. 14 I will be his Father, and he shall be My son. If he commits iniquity, I will chasten him with the rod of men and with the blows of the sons of men. 15 But My mercy shall not depart from him, as I took it from Saul, whom I removed from before you. 16 And your house and your kingdom shall be established forever before you. Your throne *shall be established forever.""" 17 According to all these words and according to all this vision, so Nathan spoke to David.*

Jeremiah 33:17-21 *"For thus says the Lord: 'David shall never lack a man to sit on the throne of the house of Israel; 18 nor shall the priests, the Levites, lack a man to offer burnt offerings before Me, to kindle grain offerings, and to sacrifice continually.'" 19 And the word of the Lord came to Jeremiah, saying, 20 "Thus says the Lord: 'If you can break My covenant with the day and My covenant with the night, so that there will not be day and night in their season, 21 then My covenant may also be broken with David My servant, so that he shall not have a son to reign on his throne, and with the Levites, the priests, My ministers.*

The Gospel according to St Matthew

The Gospel written by St Matthew was written to convince Jews that Jesus was their promised Messiah and this Gospel has been called "The Gospel for the Jews." The prophecies Matthew emphasises, are particularly linked to the deliverance of Israel as a nation. As such, Matthew's Gospel makes extensive use of Jewish tradition and references to prophecies fulfilled in the life of Christ which draw from the Tanakh or canon of the Hebrew Bible, also called the Miqra or Masoretic Text.

Elsewhere (as in the other Gospels), we see the phrase "Kingdom of God" used. In Matthew, by contrast, we see the phrase "Kingdom of Heaven"; much more familiar (and acceptable) to Jewish readers. The Gospel of Matthew calls Jesus the "Son of David" more times than any other, and also reports Jesus using the words "the House of Israel" as the focus of his mission. While aimed broadly as a Jewish audience, the Gospel according to

Matthew is also the most critical of the Jewish Leaders during the life of Christ, and particularly of those involved in His arrest, accusation and crucifixion. As such, this gospel has also been blamed for feeding into the latent anti-Semitism of some early church leaders who began to characterise the Jews as "Christ killers". However, Matthew reserves his blame for the crucifixion of Jesus for a segment of the leaders in Israel at the time, and does not blame the entire nation. Also clearly, Christ has to die for our sins and then rise from the dead, that we might be saved.

Matthew sets out to prove that Jesus is the Christ of Israel and portrays him as the Son of Abraham, and the son of David. The Gospel writer given us what seems to be a stylized version of the genealogy or bloodline of Christ, with fourteen generations from Adam to David and fourteen generations from David to Christ. On closer inspection however, we see there could be some reasons for the "style" and the apparent omissions. Some of the kings Matthew omits (for example) are those who deviated from the standards of worship and holiness required by the God of Israel and committed idolatry with other Gods. Are they "struck from the record"?

Unlike Matthew, Luke starts from Adam and traces the bloodline of Christ through a son of David called Nathan, and eventually to St Joseph who was betrothed to the Mary the Virgin Mother of Christ.

> ***Luke 3:23-38*** *Now Jesus Himself began His ministry at about thirty years of age, being (as was supposed) the son of Joseph, the son of Heli, 24 the son of Matthat, the son of Levi, the son of Melchi, the son of Janna, the son of Joseph, 25 the son of Mattathiah, the son of Amos, the son of Nahum, the son of Esli, the son of Naggai, 26 the son of Maath, the son of Mattathiah, the son of Semei, the son of Joseph, the son of Judah, 27 the son of Joannas, the son of Rhesa, the son of Zerubbabel, the son of Shealtiel,*

the son of Neri, 28 the son of Melchi, the son of Addi, the son of Cosam, the son of Elmodam, the son of Er, 29 the son of Jose, the son of Eliezer, the son of Jorim, the son of Matthat, the son of Levi, 30 the son of Simeon, the son of Judah, the son of Joseph, the son of Jonan, the son of Eliakim, 31 the son of Melea, the son of Menan, the son of Mattathah, the son of Nathan, the son of David, 32 the son of Jesse, the son of Obed, the son of Boaz, the son of Salmon, the son of Nahshon, 33 the son of Amminadab, the son of Ram, the son of Hezron, the son of Perez, the son of Judah, 34 the son of Jacob, the son of Isaac, the son of Abraham, the son of Terah, the son of Nahor, 35 the son of Serug, the son of Reu, the son of Peleg, the son of Eber, the son of Shelah, 36 the son of Cainan, the son of Arphaxad, the son of Shem, the son of Noah, the son of Lamech, 37 the son of Methuselah, the son of Enoch, the son of Jared, the son of Mahalalel, the son of Cainan, 38 the son of Enosh, the son of Seth, the son of Adam, the son of God.

Matthew by contrast only begins with Abraham and traces the lineage from King David through King Solomon and Jeconiah and then again on to Joseph

Matthew 1:1-17 *The book of the genealogy of Jesus Christ, the Son of David, the Son of Abraham: 2 Abraham begot Isaac, Isaac begot Jacob, and Jacob begot Judah and his brothers. 3 Judah begot Perez and Zerah by Tamar, Perez begot Hezron, and Hezron begot Ram. 4 Ram begot Amminadab, Amminadab begot Nahshon, and Nahshon begot Salmon. 5 Salmon begot Boaz by Rahab, Boaz begot Obed by Ruth, Obed begot Jesse, 6 and Jesse begot David the king. David the king begot Solomon by her who had been the wife of Uriah. 7 Solomon begot Rehoboam,*

Rehoboam begot Abijah, and Abijah begot Asa. 8 Asa begot Jehoshaphat, Jehoshaphat begot Joram, and Joram begot Uzziah. 9 Uzziah begot Jotham, Jotham begot Ahaz, and Ahaz begot Hezekiah. 10 Hezekiah begot Manasseh, Manasseh begot Amon, and Amon begot Josiah. 11 Josiah begot Jeconiah and his brothers about the time they were carried away to Babylon. 12 And after they were brought to Babylon, Jeconiah begot Shealtiel, and Shealtiel begot Zerubbabel. 13 Zerubbabel begot Abiud, Abiud begot Eliakim, and Eliakim begot Azor. 14 Azor begot Zadok, Zadok begot Achim, and Achim begot Eliud. 15 Eliud begot Eleazar, Eleazar begot Matthan, and Matthan begot Jacob. 16 And Jacob begot Joseph the husband of Mary, of whom was born Jesus who is called Christ. 17 So all the generations from Abraham to David are fourteen generations, from David until the captivity in Babylon are fourteen generations, and from the captivity in Babylon until the Christ are fourteen generations.

The Gospels of St Matthew and St Luke

We may need to say a few words about the apparent disparities between the accounts given by St Matthew and St Luke. It is possible that some of problems in the comparison of the accounts actually refer to forms of Levirate Marriage. Another viewpoint is that the differences in the two lineages by Luke and Matthew can be explained by theories that Matthew gives us the lineage of Christ through Joseph his foster father, while Luke gives us the lineage through the Holy Virgin Mary. Eli is her father, and in Luke's account Jesus is possibly being described as a son (grandson) of Eli who is supposed by many to be the son of Joseph, simply because Mary could not be put down as a lineage in her own right for cultural reasons, and the attitude to women at that time. A few have claimed that Matthew rather than Luke gives the lineage of Christ through the Virgin Mary, but here we presume that it is Luke who actually does this.

It is more plausible that Luke is giving us the Virgin Mary's account of the Gospel as he has details that would have come from her, or at least from the viewpoint of a woman who had been close to the earthly life of Christ from His birth. There is internal evidence within the Gospel of Luke, which may well support that claim of Mary being the major source for much of the information found only in that Gospel.

Matthew, Mark and John give us scant detail of Mary the Virgin Mother of our Lord, especially her thoughts, feelings and reactions to the events of the Gospel accounts. Luke on the other hand seems to have some special insight and perhaps some first-hand information about her. Only Luke portrays the Virgin Mary as a fully active participant in the unfolding drama of Redemption. He alone gives us the intimate details of Zachariah and Elizabeth and the relationship between Elizabeth and Mary her young cousin. Only the Gospel of Luke gives us the unique flashes of insight into Mary's response to the Annunciation by the Angel, the rejoinder of her prophetic hymn (the Magnificat). This is the only Gospel that gives us the details of the presentation of Jesus in the Temple; and the encounter with the Prophet Simeon and the Prophetess Anna (the first evangelist).

There is therefore a fair bit of internal evidence that the Virgin Mary could have been a major source for the writing of St Luke's Gospel account, and some traditional stories in the heritage of the ancient church seem to support this. Modern revisionist theologians however try to discount this Marian influence on the writing of St Luke, and they raise doubts and controversies about several aspects of the genealogies. We can also discount the addition of the name Panthera into the genealogies by certain Jewish and other writers as deliberately misleading and highly contradictory in the so-called evidence presented.

Matthew's genealogy appears to be "representational" with 42 generations divided into three sets of fourteen. There are a number of "omissions" and "name changes" that are not pertinent to our study here, save to say that there appears to be a reasoning behind the schematics of Matthew's genealogy. For example the three kings of Judah Ahaziah, Jehoash, and Amaziah who are left out of the list, are from the line of Ahab which was "cursed", and they each came to a bad end after rebelling against God.

Our purpose here is not to deal with those arguments about the differences in these two accounts, but to show those recorded in the lineage or blood-line of Christ who intermarried with or were otherwise related by blood to Ham the progenitor of Africans in the Bible. We shall also look at those in the blood-line of Christ (and their associates) who interacted with Africa or Africans in any significant way, such as helping to preserve that precious blood-line for the Saviour to be born according to Bible prophecy! Beyond that, we shall also occasionally see other interactions between Africa and Israel for example.

Christ's Genealogy in Luke's Gospel

In his genealogy or bloodline of Christ, St Luke traces the lineage from God to Abraham like this, by excluding the line of Cain who of course is famous for murdering his brother Abel:

1. Adam
2. Seth
3. Enosh
4. Kenan
5. Mahalalel
6. Jared
7. Enoch

11. Shem
12. Arphaxad
13. Shelah
14. Eber
15. Peleg
16. Reu
17. Serug

8. Methuselah	18. Nahor
9. Lamech	19. Terah
1(Noah	20. Abraham

From Noah forward, the lineage in Luke's Gospel is clearly Semitic. We will go on to see that this mainly Semitic bloodline, had a number of very significant interactions with another Hamitic or African line also descended from Noah. *We will also prove that Africa helped to save the blood line that produced the Christ!* The Semitic line that produces Christ, depends on the Hamitic or African line repeatedly through history and there are places and points in that story, where the Semitic line of Christ would probably not have survived without the help of their Hamitic cousins. This book shows how the interactions between the descendants of these two children of Noah, Shem and Ham sometimes becomes crucial to the fulfilment of God's plan!

We will however also see that race or ethnicity in the Bible becomes based more on lineage or descent, rather than identity based on physical appearance. This is another reason why Bible names are therefore often qualified mainly by paternal ancestry. Names in the Bible also often contain a clue as to ancestry. Examples are scattered throughout scripture and a few are given below.

- Ephron the son of Zohar (the Hittite)

- Joshua the son of Nun

- Laban, son of Bethuel (the Syrian)

- Lot the son of Haran

- Mahalath the daughter of Ishmael, Abraham's son

- Saul the Benjamite

- Saul the son of Kish

- Shechem, the son of Hamor the Hivite

- Uriah the Hittite

- Jesus Christ himself is often referred to as the Son of David.

This patrilineal practice however also means that the entry of other ethnicities into lineage lines (through marriage for example) can sometimes be blurred; as (importantly) <u>the name of the father is usually given</u> rather than that of the mother. The same type of patrilineal origin (or progenitor based identity), is also applied to physical objects such as the Ark of Noah, the Tabernacle (Moses), or the First Temple (Solomon). "The Table of the Nations" in Genesis Chapter 10 is similarly organised according to patrilineal descent of families or genealogy, rather than language or physical appearance as the earth is re-populated after the Great Flood.

Chapter Three –The Flood of Noah

We now return to the great Flood of Noah which is the real beginning of the story of the sons of Ham. Can we believe the Bible story of the Great Flood and the Ark of Noah? Could the Ark have been large enough? The story of the Ark and the Flood of Noah become simpler if the numbers of the species on the Ark are reduced simply to "kinds" just as the Bible says.

The animal and human survivors of the Ark were probably able to migrate easily, because the geography on the Earth may have been different to what we know see and know.

Evolutionists are of course welcome to have their opinion, but for the purpose of our study here, we will take the timeline of the Bible literally. There is good reason to take the Bible accounts more seriously than some of the imagination and speculation that passes as "science" especially on television. For example, several strata (layers of rock) that some claim were laid down over millions of years, actually appear to have been deposited quite suddenly. That is why we still find huge numbers of fossils that were obviously buried quickly while still alive, during an event like a Great Flood . It is actually logical that many aspects of the Earth are much younger than they appear. Carbon dating is also often nowhere near as accurate as sometimes made out to be.

The vast resources spent on the theory of evolution, have also failed to show evidence of any new species and only show changes within species. The missing link is missing and the huge amounts spent on finding life in outer space, could be better used to feed the poor and provide for others in need.

The 370 days of the Flood story in Chapters 6–9 of Genesis, are depicted as a divine judgement for human sin, which finally ends the line of Cain. This could be seen in some ways a return to the original flood before creation (Gen 1:2), and humanity starts again with the family of Noah. Animal life begins afresh with the cargo from the Ark. Fish and other deep sea creatures probably just kept on swimming through the whole episode...

There have long been stories of sightings of "the remains of Noah's Ark", some of these in Armenia or nearby countries. We do not need to see the Ark to believe that it could very well have existed. While there have been some of these stories of sightings that could bear further investigation, several have been found to be hoaxes. The dilemma is not helped by the fact that the area of Armenia in question is apparently a Military Reserve. Robert Ballard who found the wreck of the Titanic, claims to have found some evidence of a great flood around the Black Sea, that supports earlier theories by scientists at Columbia University. Ballard's findings are so far not sufficient to prove or disprove the story of Noah's Flood in the Bible. Similarly, speculation of the relationship between this story and other flood stories does not really prove anything either way.

Many Christians point out that Jesus Christ and His Apostles accepted the story of the Flood of Noah as true and that is sufficient for them to believe it too.

> **Matthew 24:37** *But as the days of Noah were, so also will the coming of the Son of Man be.*

> **Luke 17:26** *And as it was in the days of Noah, so it will be also in the days of the Son of Man:*

> **Hebrews 11:7** *By faith Noah, being divinely warned of things not yet seen, moved with godly fear, prepared an ark for the saving of his household, by which he condemned the world and became heir of the righteousness which is according to faith.*

> **1 Peter 3:20** *who formerly were disobedient, when once the Divine longsuffering waited in the days of Noah, while the ark was being prepared, in which*

a few, that is, eight souls, were saved through water.

__2 Peter 2:5__ and did not spare the ancient world, but saved Noah, one of eight people, a preacher of righteousness, bringing in the flood on the world of the ungodly;

As we shall see, **Noah was the ancestor of the Hamitic people including Mizraim, Cush and Canaan.** What does the Bible tell us about Noah? It describes him as possibly the only "truly righteous man" alive at that time, who builds the Ark in obedience to God, and then survives with his family along with the animal species they had rescued. Unfortunately shortly after surviving the Flood, righteous Noah then develops a "drink problem", exposes himself (while under the influence) and then gets angry with his children for finding the whole thing amusing...

Genesis 10 outlines the peoples descended from Noah's sons Shem, Ham, and Japheth after The Flood. Of particular interest to us here are **the** *sons of Ham, Cush, Mizraim, Put, and Canaan or progenitors of the Hamitic peoples of the Bible.* As discussed elsewhere in this book, one of those from the line of Cush was Nimrod, who built Babel and other cities in the land of Shinar. He also built or founded other cities in Assyria including Nineveh. Others who came from the line of Ham through Mizraim, were the Philistines and the Caphtorim. From this we also know that the original Philistines were not Arabs.

Another Hamitic line was through Canaan and were the families of the Sidon and Heth; as well as the Jebusites, Amorites, Girgashites, Hivites, Arkite, Sinites, Arvadites, Zemarites, and the Hamathites. The territories of the Canaanites included Sidon near Gerar, Gaza, Sodom, Gomorrah, Admah, and Zeboiim, as far as Lasha.

So in early Bible times, the Hamitic peoples occupied most of what today is North Africa, the Middle East and certainly as far as Babylon and well beyond. There are historic records indicating that Black Kings ruled long ago in parts of modern Iran. These Hamitic peoples have also been accused of being the "originators" of idolatry. That is untrue. In fact as we shall see, several Hamitic or Cushitic peoples clearly retained knowledge of the One True God.

Not all Hamitic people were Black and some eventually spoke Semitic rather than Hamitic languages, leading some scholars to conclude that the terms Hamitic or Semitic may not be as clear as had been thought. However as most of the Hamitic people live in warmer climates they are generally acknowledged to have developed the dark pigmentation associated with these climates.

Of all the various Hamitic Peoples, only the line of Canaan carried the prophetic curse of Noah who seems to have foreseen and foretold the descent of the Canaanites, into the kind of idolatry that resulted in God giving the Land of Canaan to Abraham and his descendants, to be known as Israel. Noah's "curse" was to the youngest son of

Ham. God had already blessed Ham (Gen 9:1) and Noah would know better than to curse someone whom God had already blessed!

In His eternity and in His God Nature there is no beginning and there can be no end to Christ. But in His humanity there is a line that is traced. All through scripture you see that there is a line of ancestry of Christ in His humanity; that is why in the beginnings of the gospels of Mark and Luke, there is a genealogy. Now that genealogy has much to do with the understanding of the legitimacy of His claim to who He is. But that genealogy also has so much to do with Africa. Africa had an important role to play in the blood line or genealogy of Christ.

In his article "Race and Interracial Marriage: A Biblical Survey and Perspective", Thomas M. Brown, Jr. considers commentaries by previous writers and shows how the families of peoples on the earth descend from the sons of Noah; Shem, Ham and Japheth with the following table.

Japheth	Ham	Shem
⬇	⬇	⬇
Gomer	Cush	Elam
Magog	Mizraim	Asshur
Madai	Phut	Arphaxad
Javan	Canaan	Lud
Tubal		Aram
Meshech		
Tiras		

Hamitic Babylon and Mesopotamia

The sons of Ham travelled beyond Africa, and what we today call the Middle East, into Babylon and Mesopotamia and what would later be known as Persia (Iran). For example, Shinar or ancient Babylon was clearly founded by Hamitic people. In the Bible, the name Shinar always refers to

Babylon. You would have heard the story of the "Tower of Babel" built in Shinar (Babylon or Iraq today) and the scattering of people by differing languages to different parts of the earth. You will also see (from reading the Bible) that some of these children of Ham existed or lived side by side with sons of Shem. Genesis Chapter 10 tells us that Nimrod was King of Shinar and the Tower of Babel was built on a great plain in Shinar. Genesis and Chronicles confirm that Nimrod was the son of Cush and therefore a grandson of Noah. Shinar or Babylon is therefore originally a kingdom founded and ruled by Hamitic or Cushitic people, although it appears that they were later joined there by Japhetic and Semitic neighbours. We shall see the significance of this later.

> ***Genesis 10:8-10*** *Cush begot Nimrod; he began to be a mighty one on the earth. 9 He was a mighty hunter before the Lord; therefore it is said, "Like Nimrod the mighty hunter before the Lord." 10 And the*

beginning of his kingdom was Babel, Erech,
Accad, and Calneh, in the land of Shinar.

In his article "Race and Interracial Marriage: A Biblical Survey and Perspective", Thomas M. Brown, Jr. concludes that the scattering of people by geography and language would have also have caused further changes in their physical characteristics, due to diet, climate and genetic inbreeding. In spite of prohibitions against ethnic or racial intermarriage in scripture, such marriages were not uncommon and several inter-ethnic marriages eventually became part of the earthly lineage or blood-line of Jesus Christ.

The Canaanites

Our study here is concerned more with the Hamitic lines, Cushitic and Canaanite interactions with the earthly ancestors of Jesus Christ and more widely with Ancient Israel. Along the way, we shall also look at some other significant actors, contacts and exchanges in this great divine drama. The Bible calls Egypt "the land of Ham" (Psalm 78:51; 105:23, 27; 106:22; 1Ch 4:40), with Mizraim being used in Hebrew as a name specific for Egypt. The Bible sometimes refers to Egyptians as "Hamites". Over time, the connections between language and ethnicity can become less clear. Some originally Hamitic people may eventually speak a Semitic language, and there are languages like Somali (Somalia) that are classed as "Afroasiatic" which are a cross between two language families.

Canaan was at least partly inhabited by African people before the Joshua led Israel back into the Land after their sojourn in Egypt and the Exodus under Moses. In the division of the land by the Tribes of Israel under Joshua, Simeon was in the south surrounded by Judah, and centred on Bathsheba. The Simeonites found pasture by travelling into Judah's territory to the area of Gedor near Hebron, south of Jerusalem. 1Cronicles 4:40 then tells us that Gedor was previously inhabited by Egyptians (Africans).

1 Chronicles 4:39-43 So they went to the entrance of Gedor, as far as the east side of the valley, to seek pasture for their flocks. 40 And they found rich, good pasture, and the land was broad, quiet, and peaceful; for some Hamites formerly lived there.

The name "Cush" is often more specific to Ethiopia (where there are also some Semitic people). However it is the Canaanites located in the Land Promised to Abraham who give their name to the Land of Canaan, and various parts of that land were named after their families. It is this Land of Canaan that becomes the core of the Land of Israel. Jerusalem for example was a Jebusite settlement before being taken in battle by King David. ***The Jebusites were descended from Canaan and are closely related to the Hamitic peoples of Africa!***

Genesis 10:15-18 Canaan begot Sidon his firstborn, and Heth; 16 the Jebusite, the Amorite, and the Girgashite; 17 the Hivite, the Arkite, and the Sinite; 18 the Arvadite, the Zemarite, and the Hamathite. Afterward the families of the Canaanites were dispersed.

In the Book of Exodus, we see that God sent Israel into Canaan to displace the Canaanite people who had shown some knowledge of the True God in the time of Abraham and Isaac, but had now descended into idolatry.

> **Exodus 3:8** *So I have come down to deliver them out of the hand of the Egyptians, and to bring them up from that land to a good and large land, to a land flowing with milk and honey, to the place of the Canaanites and the Hittites and the Amorites and the Perizzites and the Hivites and the Jebusites.*

The true curse of the Canaanites (which has been misinterpreted as the "curse of Ham" from Genesis 9:24-27), is actually a prophecy of the gifting of the Land of Canaan to the Jews (a Semitic people) as a result of the idolatry of the Canaanites who originally lived there. The curse had nothing to do with the other Hamitic people of Africa and elsewhere, but it was conveniently misinterpreted to justify the enslaving of Africans! Many Africans have also grown up believing this lie because it was passed on to them by schools or churches that they attended.

> *Genesis 11:1-9* *Now the whole earth had one language and one speech. 2 And it came to pass, as they journeyed from the east, that they found a plain in the land of Shinar, and they dwelt there. 3 Then they said to one another, "Come, let us make bricks and bake them thoroughly." They had brick for stone, and they had asphalt for mortar. 4 And they said, "Come, let us build ourselves a city, and a tower whose top is in the heavens; let us make a name for ourselves, lest we be scattered abroad over the face of the whole earth." 5 But the Lord came down to see the city and the tower which the sons of men had built. 6 And the*

Lord said, "Indeed the people are one and they all have one language, and this is what they begin to do; now nothing that they propose to do will be withheld from them. 7 Come, let Us go down and there confuse their language, that they may not understand one another's speech." 8 So the Lord scattered them abroad from there over the face of all the earth, and they ceased building the city. 9 Therefore its name is called Babel, because there the Lord confused the language of all the earth; and from there the Lord scattered them abroad over the face of all the earth.

We see from the Bible that the children (descendants) of Ham (Hamitic or African people) were "scattered" and eventually occupied lands as far as, and beyond the Tigris River, in fact to the beginnings of what today is Iran. That tells us again that concepts of Hamitic Africa and African peoples go beyond what modern geography and political correctness are trying to tell us.

Historically, the peoples that you could describe as African or closely related to Africa stretched all the way across southern Asia with the exception of one or two pockets. All of the rim of the Persian Gulf and the Indian Ocean, the whole of that southern swathe of Asia was peopled by Hamitic-African stock and it was the upheavals in these areas and the pressure from the light-skinned migrants pushing down from the north, that forced many of these peoples south, into the area which we today know, as the Sahara, and further down into the Pacific region for example.

Abraham, Isaac and Jacob... and Africa

Let's pick up the story with three ancient Hebrew Patriarchs named Abraham Isaac, and Jacob (Israel). Abraham and see how Africa starts to become an indispensable part of their story, and the story of the lineage or bloodline of Christ.

Abraham obeys the call of God at the age of 75 and starts (or rather completes) the journey to the land of his Promise where the Hamitic Canaanites are already living. He is known as Abram until a Covenant with God changes his name at the age of 99. The Covenant with God promises Abraham and his descendants a huge tract of land.

> *Genesis 15:18-21 On the same day the Lord made a covenant with Abram, saying: "To your descendants I have given this land, from the river of Egypt to the great river, the River Euphrates— 19 the Kenites, the Kenezzites, the Kadmonites, 20 the Hittites, the Perizzites, the Rephaim, 21 the Amorites, the Canaanites, the Girgashites, and the Jebusites."*

Alice C. Linsey (of jandyongenesis.blogspot.co.uk) and others claim some kind of Cushitic connection in Abraham's ancestry through intermarriage between the lines of Shem and Ham. That is possible. However according to Genesis Abraham is the son of Terah who dies in Haran before they reach the land of The Promise. Terah (Abraham's father), was the son of Nahor, who was the son of Serug and they are all descended from Arpachshad who is the son of Shem. By this account, Abraham and his family are Semitic. Linsey thinks it is however still possible that Abraham lived at the time when the Sahara was drying out and when there were consequent migration out of the Sahara to the north and south which could have led to what Linsey and others see as intermingling and intermarriage between Hamitic and Semitic peoples in the Mesopotamian area known as Chaldea, an area which may well have once been ruled by the Hamitic King Nimrod and his descendants.

Abraham's family is called out of Ur in the Chaldea, but Abraham himself is called by God while living in Harran. The Lord says to him, leave your father's house; I will give you a land which I will show you, which is the kind of promise that only God makes. So Abraham went. But after he got to the land of his Promise, the food in the land ran out and Abraham was faced with starvation.

The lineage or bloodline of Christ is in danger of extinction, but Abraham the great Hebrew Patriarch finds survival in Egypt in Africa!

> **Genesis 12:10-20** *Now there was a famine in the land, and Abram went down to Egypt to dwell there, for the famine was severe in the land. 11 And it came to pass, when he was close to entering Egypt, that he said to Sarai his wife, "Indeed I know that you are a woman of beautiful countenance. 12 Therefore it will happen, when the Egyptians see you, that they will say, 'This is his wife'; and they will kill me, but they will let you live. 13 Please say you are my sister, that it may be well with me for your sake, and that I may live because of you." 14 So it was, when Abram came into Egypt, that the Egyptians saw the woman, that she was very beautiful. 15 The princes of Pharaoh also saw her and commended her to Pharaoh. And the woman was taken to Pharaoh's house. 16 He treated Abram well*

for her sake. He had sheep, oxen, male donkeys, male and female servants, female donkeys, and camels. 17 But the Lord plagued Pharaoh and his house with great plagues because of Sarai, Abram's wife. 18 And Pharaoh called Abram and said, "What is this you have done to me? Why did you not tell me that she was your wife? 19 Why did you say, 'She is my sister'? I might have taken her as my wife. Now therefore, here is your wife; take her and go your way." 20 So Pharaoh commanded his men concerning him; and they sent him away, with his wife and all that he had (Also see Gen 20:12).

Now, here is the man who carries the Promise, who's about to die, and Africa saves him. He goes to Egypt, in Africa to find food and to find life in the midst of famine and death all around him in the land of Canaan promised to him by God. So **no Africa, no Patriarch Abraham!** Here we begin to see more of the key role that Africa will play repeatedly in the human ancestry of Christ and some major events in God's plan for humanity.

In Genesis 12, Sarai was ostensibly given to become a wife of the African (Hamitic) King of Egypt (Pharaoh) and in a similar story (in Gen 20), she is again given to the Canaanite King Abimelech. Neither of these relationships were consummated, but from this time forward, Africa will play a repeated role in the bloodline of Christ often interacting with the Hebrews as they become the Jews and as the story of human redemption unfolds.

We also see here that far from being an ignorant heathen idolater, Pharaoh knows when the God of Abraham speaks to him and knows how to obey! Like most men of his times, Pharaoh is a polygamist with several wives and possibly concubines as well. But he will not touch any woman who is married to another man, especially a Prophet of God. In an earlier book titled An Apostolic Handbook, Volume Two – we have shown how the teachings of Adam were passed down to generations.

On the website articles.sun-sentinel.com in 2012, Rabbi Avi Weiss argues that Abraham's journey to Egypt is a prophetic capsule of what his descendants will go through as Israel. Both Abraham and Israel are driven into Africa by famine. Sarah becomes a hostage to Pharaoh just as Israel will be held in bondage. Eventually, the power of God intervenes and Pharaoh is forced to let Israel go, taking riches with them. Rabbi Weiss argues that in calling Sarah his sister, Abraham is not ascribing the promise of bearing his children to her, and that the release of Sarah from the house of Pharaoh is perhaps a divine confirmation that she *will* be the mother of Abraham's children. Rabbi Weiss however notes that Abraham was given handmaids (shefakhot) to take home from Egypt and that one of these was probably Hagar who becomes the mother of Abraham's son Ishmael.

Hagar the Egyptian

Hagar was an Egyptian (African) and a handmaid (probably a slave) of Sarai. Some Jewish and Islamic writers see her as Abraham's wife. Most Christians only accept that Hagar became Abraham's "concubine". The Bible narrates that Sarah brings Hagar to Abraham as a kind of surrogate mother, to help Sarah bear a child after many years of trying herself.

> *Genesis 16:1-3 Now Sarai, Abram's wife, had borne him no children. And she had an Egyptian maidservant whose name was Hagar. 2 So Sarai said to Abram, "See now, the Lord has restrained me from bearing children. Please, go in to my maid; perhaps I shall obtain children by her." And Abram heeded the voice of Sarai. 3 Then Sarai, Abram's wife, took Hagar her maid, the Egyptian, and gave her to her husband Abram to be his wife, after Abram had dwelt ten years in the land of Canaan.*

Hagar's successful pregnancy for Abraham and the birth of her son Ishmael brings tensions between her and Sarah that continue even after Sarah herself miraculously has a son called Isaac, the son of her old age. Eventually things come to an unhappy climax and Hagar and Ishmael are sent away from the family. Many Arab tribes claim descent from Abraham through Hagar. *The original Arab nations therefore also have African ancestry!* Over time much of their ruling classes have come from invaders who have blended with the local population, taking on Arab culture and adopting Islam.

Some Jewish writers say that Hagar was Pharaoh's daughter and that Pharaoh gave Sarah his daughter Hagar as slave when Sarah was in Pharaoh's harem. The Jewish writers also say that Hagar is the same as Keturah. In this book we regard them as two different people following after the genealogies of 1 Chronicles.

Ishmael – Son of Abraham

So Ishmael the son of Abraham and Hagar is half Egyptian (African) and Ishmael also marries a wife from Egypt. The second son of Ishmael (Abraham's grandson) was named Kedar. Kedar means "mighty", "swarthy" or "black." Some writers claim this name was only in reference to the black tents used by nomadic tribes. It may well be a reference though to Kedar's African ancestry and physical appearance.

> *Genesis 25:13-15 And these were the names of the sons of Ishmael, by their names, according to their generations: The firstborn of Ishmael, Nebajoth; then Kedar, Adbeel, Mibsam, 14 Mishma, Dumah, Massa, 15 Hadar, Tema, Jetur, Naphish, and Kedemah.*

> *1 Chronicles 1:29 These are their genealogies: The firstborn of Ishmael was Nebajoth; then Kedar, Adbeel, Mibsam,*

Later we see a tribe called Kedar, first as nomads, but later as living in settles villages possibly descended from the son of Abraham and Hagar, and living East of Egypt and South of Israel.

> **Genesis 25:17-18** *These were the years of the life of Ishmael: one hundred and thirty-seven years; and he breathed his last and died, and was gathered to his people. 18 (They dwelt from Havilah as far as Shur, which is east of Egypt as you go toward Assyria.) He died in the presence of all his brethren.*

> **Psalm 120:5** *Woe is me, that I dwell in Meshech, That I dwell among the tents of Kedar!*

> **Song of Solomon 1:5** *I am dark, but lovely, O daughters of Jerusalem, Like the tents of Kedar, Like the curtains of Solomon.*

> **Isaiah 42:11** *Let the wilderness and its cities lift up their voice, The villages that Kedar inhabits. Let the inhabitants of Sela*

sing, Let them shout from the top of the mountains.

Kedar traded over long distances as far as Tyre

> *Ezekiel 27:21 Arabia and all the princes of Kedar were your regular merchants. They traded with you in lambs, rams, and goats.*

Kedar were a royal clan were also famous for their skill in warfare, especially archery

> *Isaiah 21:16-17 For thus the Lord has said to me: "Within a year, according to the year of a hired man, all the glory of Kedar will fail; 17 and the remainder of the number of archers, the mighty men of the people of Kedar, will be diminished; for the Lord God of Israel has spoken it."*

Kedar lived closer to Israel than other Arabs. Kedar was a name applied later in history to many of the nomadic Arabic tribes. Moslems trace the ancestry of their Prophet Mohammed through Kedar to Ishmael.

Keturah

Keturah was possibly a Jebusite and more probably an Egyptian (perhaps the same person called Hagar) and may have used the name Keturah after becoming an official wife to Abraham after the death of Sarah. As such she again brings the Hamitic line to the six sons she bears for Abraham of which Midian was one. Moses would later spend 40 years in the "Land of Midian" during his exile from Egypt.

Abimelech

In Genesis Chapter 20, Abraham goes to Gerar rather than to Egypt, to the court of another Hamitic-Canaanite ruler, Abimelech king of the Philistines. Abimelech is also descended from Ham the son of Noah, and may very well have been a tributary of Pharaoh. Abraham lies again about the identity of his wife Sarah and once again he is rebuked by God through an African (Hamitic)

King! We reproduce the encounter in a rather lengthy Bible quote below.

> **Genesis 20:1-18** *And Abraham journeyed from there to the South, and dwelt between Kadesh and Shur, and stayed in Gerar. 2 Now Abraham said of Sarah his wife, "She is my sister." And Abimelech king of Gerar sent and took Sarah. 3 But God came to Abimelech in a dream by night, and said to him, "Indeed you are a dead man because of the woman whom you have taken, for she is a man's wife." 4 But Abimelech had not come near her; and he said, "Lord, will You slay a righteous nation also? 5 Did he not say to me, 'She is my sister'? And she, even she herself said, 'He is my brother.' In the integrity of my heart and innocence of my hands I have done this."*
>
> *6 And God said to him in a dream, "Yes, I know that you did this in the integrity of your heart. For I also withheld you from sinning*

against Me; therefore I did not let you touch her. 7 Now therefore, restore the man's wife; for he is a prophet, and he will pray for you and you shall live. But if you do not restore her, know that you shall surely die, you and all who are yours." 8 So Abimelech rose early in the morning, called all his servants, and told all these things in their hearing; and the men were very much afraid. 9 And Abimelech called Abraham and said to him, "What have you done to us? How have I offended you, that you have brought on me and on my kingdom a great sin? You have done deeds to me that ought not to be done." 10 Then Abimelech said to Abraham, "What did you have in view, that you have done this thing?"

11 And Abraham said, "Because I thought, surely the fear of God is not in this place; and they will kill me on account of my wife. 12 But indeed she is truly my sister. She is the daughter of my father, but not the daughter of my mother; and she became my wife. 13 And it came to pass, when God caused me to wander from my father's house, that I said to her, 'This is your kindness that you should do for me: in every place, wherever we go, say of me, "He is my brother."'" 14 Then Abimelech took sheep, oxen, and male and female servants, and gave them to Abraham; and he restored Sarah his wife to him. 15 And Abimelech said, "See, my land is before you; dwell where it pleases you." 16 Then to Sarah he said, "Behold, I have given your brother a thousand pieces of silver; indeed this vindicates you[a] before all who are with you and before everybody." Thus she was rebuked. 17 So Abraham prayed to God; and God healed Abimelech, his wife, and his female servants. Then they bore children; 18 for the Lord had closed up all the wombs of the house of Abimelech because of Sarah, Abraham's wife.

We have spoken already of how Abraham the great Patriarch of the Hebrews is saved from famine by Africans. What is perhaps even more remarkable in two of these situations with Abraham, Pharaoh and Abimelech; is that *the Hamitic rulers, far from being heathen idolaters are familiar enough with the same God that Abraham worshipped!* They see God in dreams, they understand what He tells them and THEY OBEY HIM! At the same time, God shows them that Abraham is his special servant and that they are to respect and listen to him.

The Palestinians

Strangely, there is absolutely no record in history of a group of people called the Palestinians in the area known as Israel in the Bible. Not a single Assyrian, Babylonian, Persian or Greek chronicle mentions a "people" called the "Palestinians". Neither can the "Palestinians" be related to the "Philistines" of the Bible. *Those ancient*

Philistines were clearly not Arabs. Further those Philistines were defeated by Assyria and then were assimilated into the Babylonian and Persian Empires. By the 4th Century BC, the Philistines had disappeared as a people.

Alexander the Great did not record the presence of "Palestinians" he found only Jews. The Romans fought and defeated the Jews and renamed the land Palestine as a punishment, but never recorded any "Palestinians" in the land. Arab rule of Palestine lasted about 300 years, and then it was ruled by Turks for 600 years. The Turks also left no records of the "Palestinians", even after conducting a census. Documents from the 20th Century League of Nations Commissions and UN Commissions, only have records of Jews in "Palestine". ***Though there were a few, Arabs living alongside Jews in the land, the land was never named after these Arabs and they were never known as "Palestinians".***

The Bible records that Jesus Christ was born in Bethlehem of Judea, IN JUDEA – THE LAND OF THE JEWS!

> *Matthew 2:5&6 So they said to him, "In Bethlehem of Judea, for thus it is written by the prophet:*
>
> *6 'But you, Bethlehem, in the land of Judah,*
>
> *Are not the least among the rulers of Judah;*
>
> *For out of you shall come a Ruler*
>
> *Who will shepherd My people Israel.'" (See Micah 5:2)*

Until just a few years ago, most Arab Leaders, including the King Hussein the First of Jordan, President Assad of Syria and even PLO President Yasser Arafat, had all repeatedly stated that there were no "Palestinian" people, but that **the Arabs in the region belonged to Syria and NOT PALESTINE**. The truth is that until quite recently, no self-respecting Arab would accept being called a "Palestinian", because the name "Palestinian" was ONLY USED FOR JEWS! To call an Arab a "Palestinian" until a couple of decades ago would have been regarded as a great insult, to a people who do not take insults lightly.

So the ancient records show that contrary to popular belief, there has never been a time when there were no Jews in Israel and they were the original Palestinians. The idea of the Arab "Palestinian" people is a *very* recent concept, some writers go as far as to call the idea "an invention" to cover the fact that the majority of the "Palestinians" are Arab immigrants into Israel, who cannot trace their ancestry in the land back more than a couple of generations, and to deny the Jews a claim to a homeland called Israel.

Before returning to the story of the sons of Ham shortly, it is also worth noting that there is more than enough wealth among the Arab nations to ensure that no "Palestinian" is ever in need. Perhaps it is more convenient to show them suffering in squalor and to constantly blame this on others. If that is true, that will go down in history as one of the greatest crimes against a people by their own so called leaders, several of whom have consistently failed to account for billions of Dollars and Euros donated to improve the lives of the hapless "Palestinians".

In the next chapter, we return to the genealogy of Christ from Isaac to Joseph and their interactions with Africa.

Chapter Four – From Isaac to Joseph and Africa

The name Isaac name means laughter, "he will laugh" or "one laughs". His birth to the aged Abraham and Sarah was a miracle, and Isaac was marked with favour and prophetic blessing even before conception. Isaac was chosen in preference to the African son born of Hagar (the Egyptian) as the inheritor of the Promise from God to Abraham. He was the first of Abraham's children to receive the covenant of circumcision and was destined to keep and continue the chosen bloodline of Christ, by marrying from within the extended family.

> *Genesis 24:3-4 and I will make you swear by the Lord, the God of heaven and the God of the earth, that you will not take a wife for my son from the daughters of the Canaanites, among whom I dwell; 4 but you shall go to my country and to my family, and take a wife for my son Isaac."*

> **Genesis 24:67** *Then Isaac brought her into his mother Sarah's tent; and he took Rebekah and she became his wife, and he loved her. So Isaac was comforted after his mother's death.*

Isaac survives in the sacrifice narrative on Mount Moriah in Jerusalem (as a foreshadowing of the crucifixion of Jesus Christ) and is later married to his cousin Rebekah. This marriage is specially planned to continue the "pure" line of Abraham to inherit the promise. Isaac's nature and role as a family man shows. He is a man of prayer who speaks to God for his wife to be healed of barrenness and she has twins Jacob and Esau.

> **Genesis 25:21** *Now Isaac pleaded with the Lord for his wife, because she was barren; and the Lord granted his plea, and Rebekah his wife conceived.*

Genesis 12:10 and Genesis 42:2 show us that it was normal for the Hebrews (and probably others) to go into Africa whenever there was famine in the land where they lived.

> *Genesis 12:10 Now there was a famine in the land, and Abram went down to Egypt to dwell there, for the famine was severe in the land.*

> *Genesis 42:2 And he said, "Indeed I have heard that there is grain in Egypt; go down to that place and buy for us there, that we may live and not die."*

However God stops Isaac from actually crossing into Egypt at a place called Gerar, at the court of the son of the Canaanite ruler, Abimelech King of the Philistines, whose father had met Abraham and Sarah many years before. Abimelech is the title of a line of Kings descended from Ham the son of Noah, who may have been tributaries or subjects of Pharaoh, King of Egypt.

> *Genesis 26:1-4 There was a famine in the land, besides the first famine that was in the days of Abraham. And Isaac went to*

Abimelech king of the Philistines, in Gerar. 2 Then the Lord appeared to him and said: "Do not go down to Egypt; live in the land of which I shall tell you. 3 Dwell in this land, and I will be with you and bless you; for to you and your descendants I give all these lands, and I will perform the oath which I swore to Abraham your father. 4 And I will make your descendants multiply as the stars of heaven; I will give to your descendants all these lands; and in your seed all the nations of the earth shall be blessed;

Just as with his father Abraham in Genesis 20, Gerar becomes that place where Rebekah (like Sarai or Sarah) is given as a potential wife to the Canaanite-African King. Just as with Abraham and Sarah, Rebekah is released back to Isaac her husband. In the situation with Isaac, God does not appear in a dream to the younger Abimelech. This time, Isaac is caught in a moment of tenderness with Rebekah his wife that makes clear she is not his sister. Once again, however the Hamitic rulers are shown as men of integrity, honour and righteousness in their dealings with the Hebrew Patriarchs. Here again, the Patriarch Isaac gains wealth in his relationship with his Hamitic neighbours and envy over this causes tensions with the ordinary Hamitic people more than with the rulers. The story of Isaac, Rebekah and Abimelech is told in Genesis 26:6-11, quoted below.

Genesis 26:6-11 So Isaac dwelt in Gerar. 7 And the men of the place asked about his wife. And he said, "She is my sister"; for he was afraid to say, "She is my wife," because he thought, "lest the men of the place kill me for Rebekah, because she is beautiful to behold." 8 Now it came to pass, when he had been there a long time, that Abimelech king of the Philistines looked through a window, and saw, and there was Isaac, showing endearment to Rebekah his wife. 9 Then Abimelech called Isaac and said,

"Quite obviously she is your wife; so how could you say, 'She is my sister'?" Isaac said to him, "Because I said, 'Lest I die on account of her.'" 10 And Abimelech said, "What is this you have done to us? One of the people might soon have lain with your wife, and you would have brought guilt on us." 11 So Abimelech charged all his people, saying, "He who touches this man or his wife shall surely be put to death."

When he died at 180, Isaac was the only Patriarch who did not leave Canaan and his whose name remained unchanged. Jacob was Isaac's younger son who gains the birth-right of the eldest, in controversial circumstances that reveal the differences in preferences between Isaac and Rebekah over their children, and the strength of Rebekah in ensuring that her preferred son Isaac, inherited seniority in the family from Isaac (rather than his older twin brother Esau).

Jacob and Africa

Jacob means heel or leg "puller". He has a complex, often controversial life in which he repeatedly overcomes adversity and is remembered as the 3rd great Patriarch of the Hebrews. Jacob, the son of Isaac and Rebekah is the next link in the chain of the lineage or bloodline of Christ. God eventually renews the Covenant with Jacob, changing his name to Israel. Jacob has 12 sons Reuben, Simeon, Levi, Judah, Dan, Naphtali, Gad, Asher, Issachar, Zebulun, Joseph, and Benjamin (who father the 12 Tribes of Israel) and at least one daughter Dinah.

Israel means a wrestler, a strong person who rules by the power they have proved and the authority they have earned or are recognised to have (Genesis 32:28-29). Jacob then becomes Israel, the last of the three great Hebrew Patriarchs and his sons become the heads of the 12 Tribes of Israel.

Genesis 32:28-29 And He said, "Your name shall no longer be called Jacob, but Israel; for you have struggled with God and with men, and have prevailed." 29 Then Jacob asked, saying, "Tell me Your name, I pray." And He said, "Why is it that you ask about My name?" And He blessed him there.

Genesis 35:10 And God said to him, "Your name is Jacob; your name shall not be called Jacob anymore, but Israel shall be your name." So He called his name Israel.

As usual our main interest will be to see what interactions Jacob (and his sons) have with Africa and the other branches of the descendants of Ham, especially anything that helps to preserve and continue the bloodline of Christ. We will skip over Dan, Napntali, Gad, Issachar, Zebulun and Benjamin, since we have no reliable information about their interaction with the Hamitic lines (other than the probability of the natural necessities of trade etc.) until we deal with the entire family entering Africa later.

With Reuben, we will "ignore" his purported adultery with Bilhah his father Jacob's concubine for now, and concentrate more on Reuben's relationship with Joseph. It is Reuben who effectively saves Joseph's life and effectively allows him to be sold into slavery (rather than be killed) and eventually arrive in Egypt. Reuben also appears to have the greatest remorse over the crime he and his brothers have committed both against Joseph and their father Jacob (Israel). Unknown to Rueben and his siblings, in sparing Joseph's life, they have effectively spared their own lives and ensured that the future of the nation of Israel will be comprehensively linked with Africa and Africans!

Simeon and Africa

In the aftermath of the defilement of his sister Dinah by Shechem, the Prince of the local

Canaanite tribe (Gen 34), Simeon and Levi (presumably assisted my others unnamed) killed Shechem, his father Hamor and other Canaanite men and took the women and children captive. These were brutal times...

> **Genesis 34:25-31** *Now it came to pass on the third day, when they were in pain, that two of the sons of Jacob, Simeon and Levi, Dinah's brothers, each took his sword and came boldly upon the city and killed all the males. 26 And they killed Hamor and Shechem his son with the edge of the sword, and took Dinah from Shechem's house, and went out. 27 The sons of Jacob came upon the slain, and plundered the city, because their sister had been defiled. 28 They took their sheep, their oxen, and their donkeys, what was in the city and what was in the field, 29 and all their wealth. All their little ones and their wives they took captive; and they plundered even all that was in the houses.*

30 Then Jacob said to Simeon and Levi, "You have troubled me by making me obnoxious among the inhabitants of the land, among the Canaanites and the Perizzites; and since I am few in number, they will gather themselves together against me and kill me. I shall be destroyed, my household and I." 31 But they said, "Should he treat our sister like a harlot?"

This greatly distresses Jacob who till now had a good relationship with the local Canaanite people; who had allowed him to place his altars and worship God there. Jacob takes the entire family off to Bethel to worship God. Jewish sources however tell us that Simeon kept one of the Canaanite (Hamitic) women named Bonah to be his wife. There is also a tradition that Simeon symbolically married Dinah to try to remove the stigma of rape from her, but that they therefore lived together only as brother and sister.

Jewish Rabbinical writings also claim that Simeon was the boldest and most impetuous of Jacob's sons, big, strong for his age, and completely fearless. According to them, it was Simeon who particularly hated Joseph and he was the first to suggest that something needed to be done to get rid of him. It is interesting that Joseph meeting his brothers again (and now) as a ruler of Egypt took Simeon in particular hostage, until Benjamin was brought to him.

Levi, Judah, Shua and Tamar

As noted above, Levi joins Simeon in leading the revenge attacks on Shechem and the other local Canaanites. When Jacob lies dying, he prophesies that both Simeon and Levi's descendants will be scattered among the rest of Israel. We will see something of the implication of the scattering of the Levites later.

Judah also helps preserve Joseph's life by noticing an approaching Ishmaelite (Midianite) caravan and suggesting that Joseph be sold to them rather than killed (Gen. 37:26-28).

In Genesis 38 1 we read that Judah had a Canaanite (African) wife. She was the daughter of a Canaanite named Shuah and Judah met her while way from his brother (the other sons of Jacob) visiting a Canaanite friend "a certain Adullamite, named Hirah". Judah then has three sons who are of mixed Hebrew and Canaanite (African) stock, from this marriage Er, Onan and Shelah. The marriage of Judah to this Canaanite woman has at least two consequences pertinent to our present study, which once again show the closeness and connections between the earthly lineage of Christ and the children of Ham.

Firstly, the two older sons of Judah's marriage to the unnamed Canaanite woman called Er and Onan, both die young as a consequence of God's anger against their actions. Tamar, who had been wife to both of them then bears twins for Judah in strange circumstances, and one of those twins called Perez is listed in the bloodline of Christ. The second consequence is that Judah introduces another Canaanite or African related line into the family of Israel. In Genesis 38:5 we read that the Canaanite wife of Judah had a third son who was named Shelah, who was born at Chezib. In 1Chronicles 4:21 we see that Shelah is listed as a clan; or the family of one of the sons of Judah in the tribe of Judah. This proves again that the intermarriage between Israel and the children of Ham was not limited to Moses and Jacob, and the Hamitic lines were always part of God's plan and became part of God's people Israel.

Asher and Africa

Asher's first marriage was to an Ishmaelite woman named Adon who was directly descended from Ishmael himself, in fact Adon was Ishmael's great-granddaughter! Ishmael you would remember was the son of Abraham and the Egyptian Lady called Hagar.

Joseph and Africa

Apart from Moses, Joseph is perhaps the most influential of all the Hebrews in our story of the connections between the genealogy or bloodline of Christ and the African descendants of Ham. Joseph is also the connection between the older Patriarchs (Abraham, Isaac and Jacob) and the formation of the nation of Israel and their subsequent dramatic escape to freedom under Moses. We have seen the involvement of Joseph's brothers in his kidnap and sale to a group of travelling Ishmaelites (Midianite) traders. Today we remember the Midianites as slave traders, but we can note that they were also the means by which Joseph could reach Egypt and eventually the lineage of Christ could be saved.

The Midianites eventually sell Joseph as a slave in Egypt and he starts work in the house of Potiphar who fortuitously is the most senior military officer of the Palace Guard of the Pharaoh! The story of Joseph in Egypt takes several twists and turns that are not our main story here. Through a miraculous series of events, Joseph rises to a position of great prominence in Egyptian life, becoming the Grand Vizier or Prime Minister of Egypt, second only to Pharaoh himself. Jacob receives an Egyptian name and marries Asenath, the African daughter of Potiphera priest of On. There has been speculation that Potiphera is in fact the same Potiphar who had bought Joseph as a slave on his arrival in the country! Asenath and Joseph have two sons Ephraim and Manasseh who become the African wing of the Family of Israel.

Joseph's promotion in Egypt coincides with another even more severe famine in Canaan, the Land of Abraham's Promise. Jacob who has waited many years in what seems a forlorn hope of finding his son Joseph alive or at least finding a body to bury, sends his other sons into Egypt in Africa in search of food. They are initially unaware that the Egyptian ruler they meet in Africa is their long-lost brother! There must have been very little difference in appearance between the Hebrews and the Egyptians.

After an eventual and painful reconciliation of Joseph and the brothers who had sold him into slavery, Jacob and the entire Hebrew family move into Egypt in Africa, simply to survive. After being reunited with his lost son Joseph, Jacob lives on in Africa for another 17 years before he dies, but not before he has blessed the two African sons of Joseph, Ephraim and Manasseh, making them part of Israel and Joseph then leads the whole family along with Egyptian friend's colleagues in government and sympathisers, to bury Jacob in the cave of Machpelah, that their forefather Abraham bought from the Hittites. The massive Egyptian (African) funeral procession, with their stately ceremonial mourning procedures, apparently made a huge impression on the local African Canaanites.

Joseph also insisted on being buried back in the Land of their Promise. During the Exodus, Moses would take the remains of Joseph and probably other Hebrew Elders back across the Red Sea and then sent them on with Joshua into Israel. In the next Chapter, we look at the life and times of Moses, the African Prince.

Chapter Five – Moses the African Prince

Exodus Chapters 1-4 tell us the story of Moses, the African Prince chosen by God to lead the new nation of Hebrews out of Egypt, to form them into the nation of Israel at Sinai and send them on into their Promised Land under Joshua. Let's set the scene...

The Hyskos Theory

Some history speculates that the arrival of a new Semitic Egyptian aristocracy called the Hyskos in around 1730BC, changed the fortunes of Abraham's Hebrew descendants in Africa. This however begs the question as to why Semitic rulers would enslave the Semitic Hebrews. According to this theory, the Hyskos are eventually driven out and then the native Egyptians also turn on the Hebrews. This extended season of persecution in contrast to their former privileged status, leads the Hebrews to call on God for deliverance which God sends in the form of Moses.

The whole episode of Egyptian residence for the descendants of Abraham looks rather odd as they are effectively outside the Land of their Promise for many generations. Perhaps Egypt in Africa was also a hiding place for the Hebrews protecting them from wars in Canaan at a time when they were still few and allowing them the opportunity to grow in numbers and identity before returning to claim the promise of Abraham. Prosperity in Egypt followed by persecution had caused them to see themselves a single people or nation rather than disconnected tribes.

> **Exodus 1:7** *But the children of Israel were fruitful and increased abundantly, multiplied and grew exceedingly mighty; and the land was filled with them.*

At the time of the Exodus under Moses, the other nations that had been fighting to occupy Canaan were diminished politically and militarily; and Israel would have a chance to get established. ***God had effectively used Africa to preserve the children of Abraham, Isaac and Jacob*** till they had now grown to almost 2 million people, including 600,000 adult men able to take to the battlefield! God has also kept them away from the Land until the sin of the Canaanites and particularly the Amorites had reached the levels requiring divine retribution by expulsion from the land.

> ***Genesis 15:16*** *But in the fourth generation they shall return here, for the iniquity of the Amorites is not yet complete."*

Africa, the Sanctuary of Israel

Today we remember more of the stories of Israel suffering in Egypt. But there is another story, less often told, of how Africa originally became their sanctuary, a place of shelter, protection and prosperity for them; so much so that it took a time of persecution to remind the Hebrews of the promises of the Covenant of Abraham, and only then did they cry out to God for deliverance! This is the platform in history onto which Moses strides. However, the mistreatment of the Hebrews in Egypt, especially the behaviour of the Pharaohs "who did not know Joseph" was the beginning of the downfall of the Egyptian Empire. No nation or people survives cursing the children of Abraham whom God blessed when he said to Abraham:

> ***Genesis 12:3*** *I will bless those who bless you, and I will curse him who curses you; And in you all the families of the earth shall be blessed."*

Modern Germany is an example of a nation that rose again after making physical reparations to Jews (though more property still needs to be returned) and the spiritual exercise of repentance that was led by prophetic intercessors. Some of the African Traditional Rulers who have followed the path of spiritual reconciliation with descendants of the Enslaved Africans (as in some parts of

Ghana and South Eastern Nigeria) have also seen remarkable change and to growth and prosperity in their domains.

This ancient history of sanctuary in Africa, could also help explain why when the Ark of the Covenant was threatened in later generations, strong conjecture suggests that the Ark was secretly taken deep into Ethiopia for safe-keeping, with the son of King Solomon and the Queen of Sheba.

The Mothers and Sister of Moses

The early life of Moses is given in some detail in Exodus Chapters 2-5 and cannot be complete without the story of his mother Jochebed. This remarkable lady, a daughter (descendant) of Levi, wife to Amram and mother to Aaron and Miriam as well as Moses; is the key player in the early life of the deliverer of Israel. We get some detail of Jochebed in Exodus 2:1-10.

Exodus 2:1-10 And a man of the house of Levi went and took as wife a daughter of Levi. 2 So the woman conceived and bore a son. And when she saw that he was a beautiful child, she hid him three months. 3 But when she could no longer hide him, she took an ark of bulrushes for him, daubed it with asphalt and pitch, put the child in it, and laid it in the reeds by the river's bank. 4 And his sister stood afar off, to know what would be done to him.

Hebrews 11:23 23 By faith Moses, when he was born, was hidden three months by his parents, because they saw he was a beautiful child; and they were not afraid of the king's command.

So we see that Jochebed had something beyond motherly love almost a prophetic instinct that there was a special destiny for this child of her mature years. We find that Amram (her husband) is also in on the plan. In a dangerous defiance of a royal command for mass infanticide of all the Hebrew children, Moses is hidden for the first three months of his life. Jochebed then somehow contrives not only to have Moses rescued by the daughter of Pharaoh, but also to be hired herself as wet nurse to her own child! The Egyptian (African) Princess who rescues Moses is probably Hatshepsut the daughter of Thutmose I, who adopts him as her own son. Moses foster mother Hatshepsut, may have actually ruled Egypt for more than 20 years.

> *Exodus 2:5-10* *Then the daughter of Pharaoh came down to bathe at the river. And her maidens walked along the riverside; and when she saw the ark among the reeds, she sent her maid to get it. 6 And when she opened it, she saw the child, and behold, the baby wept. So she had compassion on him, and said, "This is one of the Hebrews' children." 7 Then his sister said to Pharaoh's daughter, "Shall I go and call a nurse for you from the Hebrew women, that she may nurse the child for*

you?" 8 And Pharaoh's daughter said to her, "Go." So the maiden went and called the child's mother. 9 Then Pharaoh's daughter said to her, "Take this child away and nurse him for me, and I will give you your wages." So the woman took the child and nursed him. 10 And the child grew, and she brought him to Pharaoh's daughter, and he became her son. So she called his name Moses, saying, "Because I drew him out of the water."

Moses Early Life and Military Career

As senior royalty, Prince of Egypt, son of the Queen, Moses lacked for nothing and was given the best education possible. Moses also received every other type of training that an African Prince of the world's greatest superpower (at that point in history) could receive. Like any Egyptian Prince of this era, Moses would have been exposed to military leadership and experience of government operations. Josephus the Jewish historian shows Moses leading the Egyptian army against an Ethiopian invasion and using innovative strategies and tactics to ensure the Egyptian victory.

> **Acts 7:22** *And Moses was learned in all the wisdom of the Egyptians, and was mighty in words and deeds.*

Josephus the Jewish historian identifies Saba with Meroe, capital of ancient Kush, a Royal City of Ethiopia, the capture of which by Prince Moses of Egypt brought him widespread fame. *According to Josephus, this new celebrity status also eventually exposed the fact that Moses was a Hebrew and not an Egyptian!* The celebration of Moses victory over Ethiopian Meroe was the beginning of his slide into exile as God prepared him for his true destiny.

At about 40 years of age, Moses sides with his people against their obvious and public humiliation by the Egyptian Rulers. It does appear that the ordinary Egyptian people were probably not that interested in the government anti-Hebrew project. For example they were still ready to lend treasure to the Hebrews, and at least some of them preferred to leave with Moses than stay with Pharaoh. In the familiar story, Moses' first attempt is to use his military skills to try and help his people, by confronting and murdering one of the Egyptian officials. Even those he is trying to help reject him and this first effort is in every way, a failure leading to his exile. Moses eventually returns and becomes the greatest prophet Priest and King that Israel would ever know until Jesus Christ was born in Bethlehem.

The descendants of Jacob (Israel) have finally remembered the saving power of the God of their great ancestors, and they cry out to Jehovah (Yahweh) for deliverance; but Israel is reluctant to accept the leader God sends them, or the methodology God chooses for their deliverance. Have you ever been in that situation where even though it's rough, you're somehow comfortable in the roughness? You got so used to the discomfort that even something better looks uncomfortable. You're complaining about where you are. You know God's calling you out of there, but you don't want to go. And so the birth pangs of Israel begin.

Exile in Midian

Moses spends 40 years in exile in Midian after this first attempt at helping his Hebrew brethren. He marries a Midianite lady named Zipporah, daughter of Jethro (Ruel) who was "Priest of the Midianites". Israel would eventually destroy the Kingdom of Midian in battle, but even then, the Hamitic line in Midian is again absorbed into Israel, through the young women "captured in battle" and who are then taken as wives by the men of Israel (Numbers 31: 17,35). Midian would remain enemies with Israel for many generations but an ancient tradition says that at least one of the wise men (Magi) who visited Jesus Christ soon after His birth was a Prince from Midian.

The forty years Moses spends in the wilderness of Midian transform him from the proud warrior prince into a humble but rugged shepherd. He learns to accept God's call rather than personal opinion and perhaps also learned many skills that would help him lead Israel through the same and similar territory, in the long Exodus from Egypt to the land of Promise. Jethro, the Midianite Priest who becomes Moses' father in law, also becomes a kind of father figure, a mentor to the fugitive from Egypt.

This phase of Moses life is a series of difficult meetings with God and with people. After an encounter with God at the "Burning Bush", and uncomfortable conversations with his brother Aaron and with Zipporah his Midianite wife, Moses sets off back to Egypt and this time, with a God-given authority and strategy rather than personal opinion, he leads the fledgling nation of Israel through a harrowing but emphatic escape out of Egypt, and then through another forty years of wanderings; before handing them over to Joshua to cross into the Land of The Promise.

Moses is an extraordinary character who still looms large over history. But all his natural gifts, life experience and God-given power and authority had not fully prepared Moses for the task of leading Israel. He was faced with repeated spiritual and vocal rebellion by the very people he was dedicated to saving. The vagaries and deprivations of life in the wilderness also took their toll on the faith of the people, as Moses had to depend on divine guidance for food, water and other provision (Exodus 16:2, Exodus 17:4).

If Africa is the womb from which Israel is born as a Nation, then the wilderness wanderings are their first formative years. They gradually learn to trust God and to obey His commandments. Out of Africa I have called my son. That's the birthing of Israel. Once more, Africa is the source of preservation for the lineages from where Christ would eventually come! Sometimes you have to leave to receive.

Birthing can be a time of stress and uncertainty. The birth pangs of Israel start and all of a sudden, Africa can't contain Israel anymore; and just like that baby being born, they have to leave to receive their Promise. Before Africa, Israel did not exist as a nation. Africa is the womb out of which Israel is born.

In Exodus 18 we see the return of Jethro (Ruel) the Midianite Priest, the adviser or mentor who seems to save Moses, from a looming, stress-related breakdown. Jethro mentors his son-in-law Moses by introducing principles of delegation in the burgeoning government of Israel. Jethro, Moses' father-in-law, had brought his daughter Zipporah and her two sons back to Moses. Jethro become a convert to the God of Israel after he hears the testimony of their deliverance from Egypt. Perhaps he was aware of the God of Moses before? He worships the Lord and is treated to a special banquet with the Elders of Israel. Observing the burden of government on Moses, Jethro advises him to leave all but the most serious matters to other appointees. Midian you will remember are descended from Abraham and his Egyptian (African) wife. Here is yet another very significant interaction between the Hamitic line and the first real leader of Israel.

> **Exodus 18:24-27** *So Moses heeded the voice of his father-in-law and did all that he had said. 25 And Moses chose able men out of all Israel, and made them heads over the people: rulers of thousands, rulers of hundreds, rulers of fifties, and rulers of tens. 26 So they judged the people at all times; the hard cases they brought to Moses, but they judged every small case themselves. 27 Then Moses let his father-in-law depart, and he went his way to his own land.*

Later, while Moses is up on the Mountain (Sinai) to bring The Law of God to Israel, it is Joshua the African (Ephraimite) he chooses to climb with rather than Aaron the Levite. On their return, they find that Aaron has been "pressured" into recreating the worship of a golden calf – something that was probably also learned in Egypt or from the practice of other nations around and within whom they were travelling. The worship of false Gods represented as cattle would become a problem again in Israel's future. On this occasion, all those who refuse to leave the idol and worship the true God of Israel are executed. Aaron is the first to repent among the Elders of Israel, and God takes the Patriarchal Priesthood of the heads of the houses and tribes in Israel away from them and creates the Levitical Priesthood.

Moses then leads the remainder in a forty-year wilderness trek in which he presides at the funerals of almost all the adults among them, who had left Egypt with him. Along the way, several of the Semitic descendants of Jacob turn against Moses (who is also an African Prince), including at one point his own sister and brother, Miriam and Aaron.

> ***Numbers 12:1*** *Then Miriam and Aaron spoke against Moses because of the*

Ethiopian woman whom he had married; for
he had married an Ethiopian woman.

Moses was prepared in Africa (and Midian) to be the man God uses to set Israel free. According to Josephus, the Ethiopian (Cushitic) wife of Moses was called Tharbis, an African Princess and the daughter of the Ethiopian King, who helped Moses enter and conquer the Ethiopian Royal city of Saba, ending the war and after which, Moses made her his wife. This is contrary to other theories that Moses married an Ethiopian woman after the death of his first wife Zipporah.

Joshua from the African (Hamitic) lineage within Israel stands by Moses in all circumstances and is rewarded as the leader of the next generation. Two others who stand out for their loyalty and faith are Hur and Caleb of the Tribe of Judah.

The "Mixed Multitude" Included Africans!

> *Exodus 12:37-39 Then the children of Israel journeyed from Rameses to Succoth, about six hundred thousand men on foot, besides children. 38 A mixed multitude went up with them also, and flocks and herds—a great deal of livestock. 39 And they baked unleavened cakes of the dough which they had brought out of Egypt; for it was not leavened, because they were driven out of Egypt and could not wait, nor had they prepared provisions for themselves.*

Who were the "Mixed Multitude"? Poor Egyptians in search of a better life, convinced by miracles of the power of the God of Moses? Or people from another Semitic group perhaps distantly related to Israel such as the Hyskos? More likely, it was a mixture of people, a combination of Egyptians, other foreigners who were then living in Egypt and perhaps particularly those who were of Semitic or mixed heritage. These would include Egyptians who were of mixed African and Hebrew ancestry; hence the Bible calls them a "Mixed Multitude". It is also possible that at least some of them were hired as mercenaries, to help defend Israel in the long march ahead. In Nehemiah Chapter 3 we see that there was a similar problem when Jews returned from Babylon.

We then need to consider what happened to this "Mixed Multitude". Where did they disappear to? If they were part of the nation that received the Law of God from Moses at Mount Sinai, could we then say that they had all immediately become Jews? From Leviticus 24:10-11 we can see that *there were Egyptians (Africans) married to Israelites and some of these had children.* Many years after the initial Exodus, there were still people in Israel who were of mixed Egyptian and Jewish heritage, who were regarded as such and apparently sometimes did not keep the Law of Moses.

Leviticus 24:10-11 Now the son of an Israelite woman, whose father was an Egyptian, went out among the children of Israel; and this Israelite woman's son and a man of Israel fought each other in the camp. 11 And the Israelite woman's son blasphemed the name of the Lord and cursed; and so they brought him to Moses. (His mother's name was Shelomith the daughter of Dibri, of the tribe of Dan.)

Some of the "Mixed Multitude" who had military or other professions were probably found useful in the new Israel. Others may have ended up as servants perhaps to the better off among the tribes of Israel. It is most likely (since we do not hear of them leaving Israel) that most of them they stayed; at least some of them converted to Judaism, intermarried and gradually disappeared into the majority population. This would be yet another significant introduction of the Cushite African lineage into the lineage of Shem and the lineage of Christ. Some others however like the Kenites joined Israel's journey only in the wilderness phase of the Exodus. Some Kenites were blacksmiths and some acted as desert guides. They were still a separate group in Israel in the time of Kings Saul and David.

> ***Judges 1:16*** *Now the children of the Kenite, Moses' father-in-law, went up from the City of Palms with the children of Judah into the Wilderness of Judah, which lies in the South near Arad; and they went and dwelt among the people.*

> ***1 Samuel 15:6*** *Then Saul said to the Kenites, "Go, depart, get down from among the Amalekites, lest I destroy you with them. For you showed kindness to all the children of Israel when they came up out of Egypt." So the Kenites departed from among the Amalekites.*

In the next chapter, we look at the lives of Aaron, Joshua, Salmon and Boaz.

Chapter Six – Aaron, Joshua, Salmon and Boaz

As we have noted, Aaron was an elder brother to Moses and became the first High Priest of Israel. We do not have much detail of interactions between Aaron and the Egyptians or other Africans. However, like Moses and Miriam, Aaron was born and raised in Africa. He was spokesman for Moses during the confrontations with Pharaoh. Aaron had his struggles with faith especially in the incident with the golden calf, and he had his other disagreements with Moses. Like Moses, Aaron dies *en-route* and is buried before Israel reaches Israel the Land of The Promise. Although we have little record of Aaron interacting with the Hamitic peoples, his grandson had an Egyptian name "Phineas", a name often used for those of African and particularly Nubian ethnicity. It is possible that Phineas just happened to be of swarthy or dark complexion. Certainly, Phineas took a particularly intense interest in fighting against interracial marriage and other interactions between Israel and any of their Hamitic neighbours.

Phinehas is remembered for his role in maintaining the religious purity of Israel and the Eastern Orthodox Churches still remember him as one of the early Saints.

Joshua and Africa

You probably already know the story of how Moses eventually hands over to Joshua, who finishes leading Israel to the land of their Promise. Joshua is described or identified as the son of Nun. As such Joshua was from an influential family in Israel.

> **Numbers 13:8** *from the tribe of Ephraim, Hoshea (Joshua) the son of Nun;*

Two of the tribes of Israel were from the descendants of Joseph, Ephraim and Manasseh. The other sons of Jacob had one tribe each. As such, Joseph received the "double portion" of the firstborn. Nun was from the tribe of Ephraim in Israel. So Joshua is descended from Joseph and his Hamitic wife Asenath, daughter of Potiphera.

Ephraim means "double fruitfulness". Joshua's father Nun, was son of Elishama and grandson of Ammihud who was one of the Elders of Israel chosen to represent Ephraim in helping Moses with governance after the Jethro the Midianite reunited Moses and his Hamitic (African) wife and family in the wilderness.

> **Numbers 1:10** *from the sons of Joseph: from Ephraim, Elishama the son of Ammihud; from Manasseh, Gamaliel the son of Pedahzur;*

Joshua's grandfather presented the gifts for the tribe's offerings when the altar was dedicated (Numbers 7:48) and led them when the tribe of Ephraim marched (Numbers 10:22). You find more of the genealogies of Israel including Ephraim in 1Chronicles Chapter 7.

We have already noted the steadfastness with which Joshua supported Moses and upheld the commandments of God. Moses had changed his name from Hoshe'a to Yehoshu'a (Joshua), probably at the time he chose him as his apprentice and successor, but the change is only reported (or made public) at the time Joshua joins the other 11 spies who go on a secret survey mission into the Land of The Promise. Hoshea (Oshea) means deliverance or deliverer Joshua (Yeshua) means Jehovah is salvation.

Yeshua is an alternative spelling and usage of the name Yehoshuah or Joshua it is also the name translated into Greek as Iesous, which through Latin becomes the English translation of Jesus. Yeshua is still preferred by Messianic Jews (who have received Jesus as Messiah), but some Eastern and Oriental Orthodox Churches prefer to use the Aramaic or Syriac translation of "Isho".

Samuel ben Meir (Rashbam) a respected French scholar of the Tosafos (medieval commentaries on the Talmud), explained the change of name as evidence of selection of Joshua as Moses' second-in-command, basing this interpretation on other changes of name by rulers of their high officials or assistants. An example of this is in Genesis 41:44-45.

> **Genesis 41:44-45** Pharaoh also said to Joseph, "I am Pharaoh, and without your consent no man may lift his hand or foot in all the land of Egypt." 45 And Pharaoh called Joseph's name Zaphnath-Paaneah. And he gave him as a wife Asenath, the daughter of Poti-Pherah priest of On. So Joseph went out over all the land of Egypt.

Israel doesn't get to the land of Promise except by the hand of the sons (and daughters) of Africa. Aaron, the first High Priest of Israel was also born and raised in Africa. God renews the covenant of Moses with Joshua, who successfully leads Israel across the Jordan River into Israel, the Land of The Promise. Joshua is responsible for ensuring that the descendants of Judah are able to settle in the land in which Jesus Christ (The expected Son of David and Son of God) will eventually be born.

Salmon and Rahab

Salmon or Salmah is listed as King David's great-great-grandfather. It is possible but unclear if his wife called Rahab (Rachab) is actually the same person who saved the Jewish spies in Jericho. According to Jewish tradition, Rahab of Jericho was married to Joshua. It could still be possible (as she was probably very young still at the time of the Jericho story) that she married Salmon later, perhaps after the death of Joshua.

> *Joshua 24:29-31 Now it came to pass after these things that Joshua the son of Nun, the servant of the Lord, died, being one hundred and ten years old. 30 And they buried him within the border of his inheritance at Timnath Serah, which is in the mountains of Ephraim, on the north side*

of Mount Gaash. 31 Israel served the Lord all the days of Joshua, and all the days of the elders who outlived Joshua, who had known all the works of the Lord which He had done for Israel.

Jericho was a Canaanite City (some writers wrongly claim it was inhabited by Semitic Amorites) at the time of Joshua's invasion, we can safely say that Rahab was a Canaanite and therefore most probably a descendant of Ham. What remains to be conclusively clarified is whether Rahab the wife of Salmon, is the same Rahab of Jericho. Her story is told in the Book of Joshua, in Chapter Two and Chapter Six.

> **Joshua 2:1-3** *Now Joshua the son of Nun sent out two men from Acacia Grove to spy secretly, saying, "Go, view the land, especially Jericho." So they went, and came to the house of a harlot named Rahab, and lodged there. 2 And it was told the king of Jericho, saying, "Behold, men have come*

here tonight from the children of Israel to search out the country." 3 So the king of Jericho sent to Rahab, saying, "Bring out the men who have come to you, who have entered your house, for they have come to search out all the country."

Joshua 6:22-25 But Joshua had said to the two men who had spied out the country, "Go into the harlot's house, and from there bring out the woman and all that she has, as you swore to her." 23 And the young men who had been spies went in and brought out Rahab, her father, her mother, her brothers, and all that she had. So they brought out all her relatives and left them outside the camp of Israel. 24 But they burned the city and all that was in it with fire. Only the silver and gold, and the vessels of bronze and iron, they put into the treasury of the house of the Lord. 25 And Joshua spared Rahab the harlot, her father's household, and all that she had. So she dwells in Israel to this day,

> *because she hid the messengers whom Joshua sent to spy out Jericho.*

We also hear about Rahab in the New Testament in the Book of Matthew Chapter One and again in the Book of Hebrews, Chapter Eleven.

> ***Matthew 1:5*** *Salmon begot Boaz by Rahab, Boaz begot Obed by Ruth, Obed begot Jesse,*

> ***Hebrews 11:31*** *By faith the harlot Rahab did not perish with those who did not believe, when she had received the spies with peace.*

Boaz and Ruth

The Jewish historian Josephus records that Boaz was a rich landowner who was a contemporary of Eli, the Priest who mentored Samuel the Prophet. Boaz notices Ruth the Moabitess working in his field, and having learned her story of loyalty to Naomi, he discretely takes care of her needs all through the harvest that year. There have been some theories put forward that the name Ephrata in connection with Bethlehem means that the people of Bethlehem (and therefore King David and Jesus Christ Himself) were Ephramites living in Judah. This book does not consider the evidence for that to be worth including here.

With some prompting from Naomi, Boaz agrees to a kind of Levirate marriage to Ruth where he pays of the debts of Elimelech and allows his family line to continue through this marriage. Boaz and Ruth have a son called Obed who in turn is the father of Jesse. The future King David is the youngest of Jesse's sons, chosen for his royal role by the Prophet Samuel.

Moab is on the east of the Dead Sea in what today is the Kingdom of Jordan. It seems that Moab and Ammon, (both sons of Lot by incestuous relationship with his daughters) and their descendants intermarried with the Canaanite peoples in the land. Thus while the language of

Moab was closely related to Hebrew, they are described both as Canaanite and as West Semitic, depending on which writer you read. The story of the origin of Moab is told in Genesis 19: 30-36 and typically for the Bible the difficult and distressing facts are fully told.

Genesis 19:30-38 *Then Lot went up out of Zoar and dwelt in the mountains, and his two daughters were with him; for he was afraid to dwell in Zoar. And he and his two daughters dwelt in a cave. 31 Now the firstborn said to the younger, "Our father is old, and there is no man on the earth to come in to us as is the custom of all the earth. 32 Come, let us make our father drink wine, and we will lie with him, that we may preserve the lineage of our father." 33 So they made their father drink wine that night. And the firstborn went in and lay with her father, and he did not know when she lay down or when she arose. 34 It happened on the next day that the firstborn said to the younger, "Indeed I lay with my father last night; let us make him drink wine tonight also, and you go in and lie with him, that we may preserve the lineage of our father." 35 Then they made their father drink wine that night also. And the younger arose and lay with him, and he did not know when she lay down or when she arose. 36 Thus both the daughters of Lot were with child by their father. 37 The firstborn bore a son and called his name Moab; he is the father of the Moabites to this day. 38 And the younger, she also bore a son and called his name Ben-Ammi; he is the father of the people of Ammon to this day.*

There is a line of thought that the Ammonites are the original Jordanians.

The Law of Moses actually forbade Israel marrying into Moabite stock. Yet Ruth does not just marry into Israel, she becomes and ancestor of Jesus Christ! In the next chapter, we look the lives of Eli the Priest, Samuel the Priest/Prophet and David the second King of Israel.

Chapter Seven – Eli, Samuel and David

Eli

Eli was a Priest and a Judge in Israel, the teacher, foster father and mentor to Samuel the Prophet (see below). Like Samuel, Eli was a descendent of Levi. Eli's two sons (who gained a reputation for corrupt lifestyles) were named Hophni and Phineas. It is unclear why Phineas had a name that appears Egyptian and even back in Africa that name was usually reserved for those of very dark appearance... For our purposes here, we must however note the major role that Eli played in training the young Samuel to hear and obey the voice of God (a story that is told in 1Samuel Chapter 3).

Samuel

Samuel is the last of the Judges and the first of the Major Prophets to the nation of Israel, as they settled into the Land of their Promise. His father Elkanah was from a Levite family in the hill country of Ephraim (we will note the significance of this shortly). Samuel is also the bridge between the time of Judges in Israel and the time of the Kings. Hugely influential, Samuel was the authority for the appointment of the first two Kings of Israel, Saul and David. Loyalties to these two kings appointed by Samuel would haunt Israel with division and civil war for many years afterwards.

Samuel's father Elkanah lived with his family in Ramah, part of an area called Zuph. Elkanah was descended from a branch of the Levites called the Kohathites. The tribe of Levi had no land in Israel, but they were attached to and lived among the other tribes for generations, providing priestly services or sometimes just leading normal lives among the people.

Samuel began to serve God very early. You may well remember the story of how Samuel's mother Hannah was unable to have a child for several years. As a wife in a polygamous home (as many were in those days) the lack of children was a source of great stigma to Hannah. She prayed to God for a child with the pledge that a child born in answer to her prayer would be given in service to God for all his life. As a result, when Samuel is born he lives only briefly with his natural parents before being fostered by Eli who allows him to live in the sanctuary at Shiloh from that early age.

> **1 Samuel 1:11** Then she made a vow and said, "O Lord of hosts, if You will indeed look on the affliction of Your maidservant and remember me, and not forget Your maidservant, but will give Your maidservant a male child, then I will give him to the Lord all the days of his life, and no razor shall come upon his head."

Let us take a leap forward in time, to a young shepherd boy called David. David is out tending the sheep and a Prophet (Samuel) shows up in his Father's house and says, get me all the sons. So they lined the boys up. He said no not this one, no not this one, no not this one. Have you not got any sons left? Oh, there's one out there tending the sheep. Go get him!

Samuel pours the oil on David, you probably know this story, but then you think for a minute who's Samuel? Samuel is the son of Elkanah and his wife Hannah. Now Hannah has no child and she dedicates whatever God will give her womb to the Lord. But you can see that Elkanah is an Ephraimite from the hills of Ephraim. He is a Levite but the families of the Levites were shared out to each of the tribes and they were part of those tribes and lived there and were part of that place for generations. Restrictions on marriage outside the Tribe of Levi only applied to the High Priest and the other Priests, and not to the entire Tribe.

Moses the Levite married women from outside Israel.

Here again we see that the Prophet Samuel emerges from the African roots of Israel. Samuel the Prophet is key to the emergence of King David. No Samuel, no King David. No King David, no Son of David. So that blind Bartimaeus can sit by the road and say, thou son of David, have mercy... It goes back to the son of the Ephrathite, who shows up with his horn of oil. Again and again and again you will see the connection between Africa and the bloodline of Christ; between Africa and the prophets of scripture.

King David

King David is the direct earthly ancestor of Jesus Christ. Most of what we know about him comes from Bible sources. Archaeology in support of the existence of King David and the ancient Kingdom of Israel is growing. For example, Dr. Avi Ofer conducted a Rank Size Index (RSI), archaeological survey in the hills of Judea, and showed that during the time of King David's reign (11th-10th centuries BC) there was a doubling in the population of the area in and around Judah, with Jerusalem at the centre of this population growth. Prof. Avraham Biran, discovered a piece of rock at Tel Dan in 1993, thought to have been a Syrian King's "victory pillar" that had been smashed later by an Israelite King. Dating to about 100 years after the time of King David, the inscriptions on the rock refer to the House or "Dynasty of David". Clay seals from the times of David and Solomon have also indicated the existence of a well organised and functioning government, centred on Jerusalem.

Discoveries in Turkey and Northern Syria also corroborate the existence of Toi, king of Hamath mentioned in 2Samuel 8:9-13. There is now growing certainty among academics about the reality of the reign of King David, although the exact borders of his kingdom are still to be determined. Moreover, the textual coherence of the Books of Kings and Chronicles in the Holy Bible however leave us with little doubt that King David is a true historical figure.

As the second King of Ancient Israel, David has a consolidating role in the geographical, cultural, religious and political life of the nation and is remembered as the greatest King of Israel. David was however a man of the times in which he lived. He was a warrior-king and although he loved God and was a great patron of the Arts, he could be as ruthless as any of his contemporaries. Both Jews and Christians expect the Throne of David to play a central role in the Last Days of the world as we now know it.

King David's African Connections

David had many connections with the Cushitic (African) peoples in his lifetime. In 1 Chronicles 11, we see that some of his closest military associates and confidants included an Ammonite (v.391, a

Hittite (v.41), and a Moabite (v.46). In 2 Samuel 18:19-30 we read that it was an Ethiopian (a Cushite) who brought the news of Absalom's death to David. Bathsheba, the mother of King Solomon, wife of King David and former wife of Uriah the Hittite commander in David's Army has been claimed by some writers as being a "Black" woman. *There is little evidence to prove that Bathsheba was a Black woman*, but she may well have had some Cushitic ancestry.

Was Bathsheba a Jewess or a Hittite like her husband Uriah? The Hittites (or Hethites) were descendants of Heth, of Canaan, Ham, and Noah. Hittites had been in the land before Abraham and although they were meant to have been destroyed for their idolatrous practices, some like Uriah remained in Israel. Uriah is most likely to have married a fellow Hittite. Interestingly, Willis Judson Beecher (1838 – 1912) thought it unlikely that King David's Counsellor Ahitophel could have been old enough to have a married daughter at the time of the King's adultery with Bathsheba, still less that

Ahitophel (if he were Bathsheba's father) would have encouraged Prince Absalom to rebel against King David and take over the throne instead of Prince Solomon, who would then have been Ahitophel's own grandchild.

Often portrayed as an adulterous seducer, Bathsheba may well be one of the most maligned women in history. It was far from unusual for women in those days to take their bath in the walled yard in the evening, and they would have been well hidden from all except the king, who alone was on such a high vantage point. They would also not have been naked as Western artists have often portrayed her, but would be wearing some clothing light enough to allow their maids to wash them down. Far from seducing King David, Bathsheba probably responds innocently to his summons, and comes to the palace perhaps hoping to hear some news of her husband who is fighting for David at the battlefront. Once alone inside the palace with the great king, the great hero and goliath-slayer, Bathsheba stood no chance against his determined advances, for his libido was probably already well aroused.

Rather than be portrayed as a wicked schemer, Bathsheba should probably be seen as a victim of circumstances who tried to keep both the king's name and that of her husband as well as her own modesty intact, in what must have been an impossible selection of choices. If her subsequent handling of delicate political situations and her legacy of wisdom teaching to her son Solomon in Proverbs 31 are taken into account, this most favoured lifelong wife of King David is certainly not the wicked woman that history (and art) has often portrayed her to be. Uriah and Bathsheba may not have been Black, but they were certainly partly descended from Ham, the "Father of the Africans". Here yet again we see the Hamitic line introduced at an important time in the story of the lineage or bloodline of Christ, for Bathsheba is the mother of the next great king of Israel, King Solomon. In the next chapter, we look at the life and times of King Solomon, his mother Queen Bathsheba and Hiram of Tyre. We also trace the origins of several ancient Jewish communities in Africa!

Chapter Eight – Solomon and Sheba

The favoured son and successor of King David and his Queen Bathsheba, was King Solomon. The young king finds his favoured wife and mother of his heir Rehoboam, in Naamah the Ammonite, the only woman out of his reported 700 wives and 300 concubines, who is recorded by name. The Bible account also shows us that many of the wives and concubines were Canaanite and possibly other Cushitic women, including at least one who was Egyptian (the daughter of a pharaoh). Although some of these "marriages" were just symbolic signs of political alliances, the presence of pagan women in the life of the King had some very serious consequences.

> *1 Kings 11:4 4 For it was so, when Solomon was old, that his wives turned his heart after other gods; and his heart was not loyal to the Lord his God, as was the heart of his father David.*

The Ammonites are descended from Ammon who along with Moab was born out of Lot's incestuous relationship with his daughters. Like Moabites, the Ammonites would have intermarried with other people in the region to build their population as this marriage with Israel also shows. The heathen gods of Moab and Ammon (especially Milcom or Molech, god of the Ammonites) were described by God as abominations. However once again we see the intermingling of Hamitic/Cushitic lines with the Semitic bloodline of Jesus Christ.

Hiram of Tyre

Compared to King David his father, Solomon had fewer military challenges from the nations around him, several of whom were preoccupied with internal problems of their own during his reign. King Solomon also had some powerful friends such as Hiram King of Tyre, who had also been friends with King David.

1 Kings 5:1 *Now Hiram king of Tyre sent his servants to Solomon, because he heard that they had anointed him king in place of his father, for Hiram had always loved David.*

Who was "Hiram, King of Tyre"? Hiram was King of the Phoenician City State of Tyre, one of the powerful and influential federation of city states on the coast of what today is the South Governorate of Lebanon. Eurocentric historians have consistently claimed that the Phoenicians and almost all other inhabitants of the "Near East" were Semitic, including all Canaanites. However we have seen earlier that the first Canaanites were Hamitic or Cushitic even though culture and language sometimes later changed to Semitic forms.

The Phoenicians were seafaring traders who travelled the entire Mediterranean. Their alphabet is the basis of Greek and other writing that followed. The ancient Phoenicians were descended from earlier Canaanites who were trading partners and allies of ancient Egypt 3000 years before Christ was born! As we have also seen earlier, these original inhabitants of the land later called Canaan were in fact the descendants of Ham and Cush.

The Queen of Sheba

Perhaps the most famous woman in the life of Solomon after his mother Bathsheba is the Queen of Sheba (called Makeda in Africa). Some European archaeologists argue that Saba was a Semitic Kingdom stretching at various times from the south of modern Saudi Arabia, through Yemen and up to Aqaba and Ethiopia. Some of their kingdom however would only be outposts to guard their trade routes and other political and financial interests. Outside the Bible, the existence of the Sabean kingdoms in these areas is confirmed by Assyrian historians and by Strabo, the Greek philosopher, geographer, and historian. In Africa, the deity or god of the Sabean kings and queens was El-Makea or El- Makua. The ancient Kingdom of Aksum (Axum), the Himyarite Kingdom of ancient Yemen, and the Sabean Kingdom of South Arabia, had been interlinked by trade, politics, military conquest and intermarriage for thousands of years. Persia (modern Iran) has also been contesting for control of Yemen and Arabia against Egypt, Ethiopia and other regional powers for many centuries.

It may be worth mentioning that in the Book of Genesis we find Sheba (Sabea) mentioned twice, once as Hamitic and secondly as Semitic. This may be due to there being two people of this name who had descendants found worthy of note by ancient writers or it may simply indicate again, the level of interaction and intermarriage between these two lineages. The Ethiopian and Yemenite traditions support this view. It could also be because of the proliferation of Sabean trading colonies that may have confused writers as to their origins and actual location.

The Jewish and later Christian Empire of Ethiopia crossed over into Yemen, Arabia and beyond at different periods of history. The Himyarite site called Ẓafār in Yemen was the ancient capital of a tribal grouping that once ruled all of today's Saudi Arabia and into Iraq from about 110BC to 525AD. Ẓafār in Yemen has been found to be the oldest of such sites and was once home to a large population of Jews and Christians! Archaeological excavations at Ẓafār have revealed the splendid statue of *an African Axumite or Ethiopian King of this Empire, wearing the crown of a Christian Emperor!* The royal lineages across this region also made alliances that were often based on marriages as the relationship between Solomon and Sheba proves.

HIH Prince Ermias Sahle-Selassie Haile-Selassie, President of the Crown Council of Ethiopia, speaking on "The Origins of the Solomonic Dynasty and The Throne of David in Ethiopia" at the DuSable Museum of African-American History, on June 29, 2014, gave some insights into Queen

Makeda of Saba, and he has kindly allowed us to use parts of his speech in this book. Prince Ermias said:

> *"The kingdom of Saba or Sheba, whose people were known as Sabaeans and whose name means Host of Heaven and Peace, rose to power during the early part of the 1st millennium BC. Situated in southwest Arabia on the eastern tip of the Red Sea in the region of present day Yemen and extended westward across the Red Sea including Ethiopia, the kingdom occupied an area of some 500,000 square miles".*

According to Prince Ermias, the Queen of Saba was also Queen of Ethiopia and Egypt (Queen of the South). She is known as Bilqus or Balkis in Arabic, Makeda, Magda, Maqda or Makera (meaning "Greatness) in Ethiopia, and was also called Nikaulis by Josephus the historian." Makeda was trained as a royal astronomer and astrologer, as was necessary for the practice of the Sabean pagan religion and the government of her kingdom. The Prince stated that the Ka'aba building at the centre of the Al-Masjid al-Haram Mosque in Mecca, Saudi Arabia still has within it a black stone, a meteorite that was once used as part of the religious worship system of pagan Sabaeans and Ethiopians. The moon goddess associated with that stone was known as Shabya who was worshipped along with another goddess called Astarte, Ashtar or Astar.

According to the sources quoted by Prince Ermias in this speech, the journey made from the Royal palaces at Aksum by the Queen Makeda of Saba to visit King Solomon in Israel was a diplomatic move to avoid a military confrontation. It resulted in her conversion to Judaism and the birth of a child to Solomon and the Queen. According to Prince Ermias:

> "A son was born to the queen from her union with Solomon. This son, Menelik I,

grew up in Ethiopia, and later during his 20s returned to Jerusalem where he spent some few years visiting with his father King Solomon, eventually returning to his own country with Solomon's 'Holy of Holies' the Ark of the Covenant".

Certainly Meroe, the capital of Ancient Kush, was also ruled from Axum by Emperor Ezana of Ethiopia, whose empire once stretched over Ethiopia, Djibouti, Eritrea, North Somalia, North Sudan, South Egypt, South Saudi Arabia and Yemen. Ezana is the Ethiopian Emperor credited with introducing Christianity as the formal or state religion of Ethiopia.

Just before Islam emerges in the 7th Century, the Arabian Peninsula suffered from a series of droughts and widespread disease, which may have contributed to the demise of the old political and religious structures in that region, and helped pave the way for the rise of Islam. This was also probably the time at which some of the Black Jews of Yemen crossed back into Africa. Others would leave as Islam took over the territory and relationships between the religions began to deteriorate.

The Ark of the Covenant

In his speech at the DuSable Museum of African-American History, on June 29, 2014, HIH Prince Ermias Sahle-Selassie Haile-Selassie, states that the entourage which escorted Menelik I on his return from visiting his father King Solomon included the son of the Levite Zadok named Azarius, and other aristocrats and intellectuals from Israel. The Ark of the Covenant came with them for safe keeping and remains at Axum till this day. Prince Ermias said:

> *"The symbolism of the Ark is of profound religious significance in the Ethiopian orthodox church. Each church must contain a replica of the Ark before it can be consecrated. One of the most important*

festivals in the calendar of the Ethiopian orthodox church is Timket, at which time the Ark or a replica thereof, is wrapped in a shroud and carried in great processional reverence".

The importance of the presence of the Ark of the Covenant in their nation to the people of Ethiopia, cannot be overestimated. As it is true that real smoke usually indicates a fire, there is every possibility that more than just a grain of truth, lies within in these ancient stories from Ethiopia. Whether the original Ark of Israel (or an offical copy) is in Axum may still be debated, but clearly there is huge religious, spiritual, cultural and political capital invested by the Ethiopians in their belief that the original Ark was brought to them long ago. It is highly unlikely that anyone, let alone these vast numbers of people over so many centuries would or could fabricate and sustain this if it were a lie, without a strong alternative narrative, emerging to contest it. The loss or disappearance of the Ark of the Covenant from

Israel has deepened and broadened the mystery, adding credibility to the Ethiopian claims. The balance of very strong probability is that someone, probably King Solomon of Israel took a strategic decision not just to link the royal lineages Jerusalem and Aksum, but also to connect the religious and spiritual destiny of the Jews and the Ethiopians of Africa!

So according to the Ethiopian historical records, when God needed a place to keep the Holy Ark of the Covenant safe, He sent it to Africa, just as He had used Africa to save the Jewish Nation and would use Africa to save Jesus Christ from being murdered as a child. In Ethiopia the ruling families have repeatedly crossed ethnic lines, in an ancient land where Cushitic and Semitic peoples have lived together for millennia, and still do today.

Over and over, we see a critical role played by the African continent in the plans of God. Although the rulers of Saba in Southern Arabia are thought of by some historians as Semitic at the time of King Solomon; it is also quite plausible that the marriage of King Solomon and the Queen of Sheba, was in fact part of a wider pattern of intermarriage between the royal families of the ancient empires in the region, similar to that practiced between the royal families of Europe into the modern era.

Beta Israel

The ancient relationships between Israel and Africa can still be seen in several other ways, even in modern times. The people known as Beta Israel (House of Israel) have been proven both by their religion and culture, and by genetic investigation, to be African Jews. They were found mainly in Tigray and Amhara in Ethiopia, but most have now been airlifted (sometimes secretly) to Israel. By contrast to those Jews in the Mediterranean area of North Africa, genetic studies show that these Ethiopian groups, are probably descended from a small group of Jews who arrived there at more than 2000 years ago, intermarried with and probably converted the naïve population. This is again consistent with the traditional history of Ethiopia which tells of a delegation of Jews sent by King Solomon who remained in Ethiopia. The Jewish Festival of Hanukkah which started only 200 years before Christ was unknown among Ethiopian Jews, but the older Jewish festivals were well known among them!

Falasha Mura

Falasha Mura, are also Ethiopian Jews, related to Beta Israel, but the Falasha have largely converted to Christianity. If they have Jewish mothers, they are also welcomed in Israel, but only if they convert to Orthodox Judaism. Messianic Jews and other Christians from Europe and America, have been making efforts to meet the medical and other needs of the Falasha Mura, who ae often among the very poor and marginalised of society where they live.

Lemba

Recent scholarship has also proved Jewish Ancestry for the Lemba people, even as far further south of Ethiopia as Tanzania, Kenya, Malawi, Mozambique, South Africa and Zimbabwe. Scholars believe that the traditions of people like the Lemba are also pre-Second Temple Israelite and have a Southern Arabian (Yemeni) and Ethiopian origin. *The story of the Lemba proves again, the ancient connections between Ethiopia, Arabia and Jerusalem!*

Other ancient African Jewish communities are very well known, such those across Mediterranean North Africa. Jews were deported from Egypt to Cyrenaica in Libya some three hundred years before Christ. When the Temple in Jerusalem was destroyed, the Roman Army also expelled over thirty thousand Jews to Tunisia. We will take only a brief look at them here.

The Maghrebi

The Maghrebi (Western) and Mizrahi (Eastern) Jews, are communities who have been part of North Africa (and the Middle East) sometimes for several thousand years. Most of them have recently been forced out of their homes in majority Moslem countries, often leaving with little or nothing of their possessions, and they are the majority of Jews in Israel. Very few of these Maghrebi or Mizrahi communities now remain outside Israel.

Sephardi

Sephardi Jews (Sephardi means Spanish in Hebrew) are mainly those who were expelled from Southern Europe, particularly Spain and Portugal after the infamous 15th Century Alhambra Decree (edict of Expulsion of the Jews) by the Catholic Monarchs of Spain. As most of the Sephardi Jews arrived into North Western Africa, their culture has largely displaced that of the Maghrebi and the two groups have largely integrated there. It is also possible that many of the Sephardi were also Maghrebi who earlier crossed over into the Iberian Peninsula. This is another example of migration out of and then back into Africa. Maghrebi, Mizrahi and Sephardi Jews have all been shown genetically to be largely distinct from their African host communities, proving that these Jews migrated into Africa. Some have been shown to have been in Africa since Bible times.

Ashkenazi

Ashkenazi Jews are those who have earlier lived in Central and Eastern Europe (Ashkenazi means "Germany" in Hebrew), and these are found more in South Africa; where they came before and after the Holocaust. Several of these South African Jews played important roles in the antiapartheid struggles there.

Other African Jews

Several Jewish communities were founded along the Trans-Sahara trade routes down to Timbuctoo and other cities on the great bend of the River Niger and along other trading routes such as the old Silk Road as far as Burma and possibly China. Historically several other Jewish groups also existed in the Bilad el-Sudan of West Africa, as well as along the coast and islands of that region around Senegal and Gambia. Researchers have claimed the possibility that groups of the Igbo, Ibibio and Annang of South Eastern Nigeria, as well as several clusters in the Cameroon might also have Jewish ancestry. However whether or not this is the case, most of these groups have certainly become non-halachic over the centuries and many are now Christian or Moslem. Even where they have provable Jewish cultural practices, they have often had no access to the Talmud and no knowledge of the later feasts such as Purim and Hanukkah.

Other historical sources recorded mainly Maghrebi Jewish Communities living in the ancient African Kingdoms of Ghana, Mali, and later Songhay empires for over eight hundred years between 790 and 1600. Some of these Jews had travelled south from Egypt through Chad. Still others were known to have come to Africa from as far away as Yemen, some originally as war captives.

As we have seen, some Jewish communities began southward migrations from Morocco (and Egypt) in North Africa, and even from Portugal after Christian persecution of Portuguese Jews. Others were seeking to move away from the increasing Islamic rule in North Africa. Many Jewish groups remained in the Sahara and in Sub-Saharan Africa even after the rise of Islam, in addition to the better known groups in Eastern Central and Southern Africa. It is quite possible that among those taken from Africa during the Slave Trade were some who were Jews or Christians. Today, almost all these Saharan Jews are gone.

Jewish Africa is a fascinating area of study and the records of Jewish communities in places like Timbuktu need to be preserved quickly before they are completely lost. DNA tracing may also reveal Jewish roots for several other African communities besides Beta Israel, Falasha Mura and the Lemba; hitherto unknown as having Jewish ancestry. There are now other emergent modern communities of more recent Jewish converts in Côte d'Ivoire, Ghana, Kenya, Nigeria, Uganda and Zimbabwe. Outside of some parts of Islamized Africa, the type of Anti-Semitism known in Europe had been rare.

In the next chapter, we read about the Kings of Israel after Solomon, such as Hezekiah, Manasseh and Amon, as well as the Prophet Jeremiah.

Chapter Nine – Kings After Solomon

Hezekiah, Manasseh, and Amon

There was not much recorded interaction between these three Kings of Israel and Africa or her descendants. However Hezekiah did have an ill-fated military alliance with Egypt. In the reign of Hezekiah, (King of the southern Kingdom of Judah) the Assyrians conquered the Northern Kingdom of Israel and from then on Judah itself was also under continuous pressure. Hezekiah, entered into an alliance with the ruling Pharaoh of Egypt against the Assyrian King Sennacherib. At the critical moment in around 701 BC, the African King let Hezekiah down leaving him to fight Assyria alone. But God came to the rescue of Judah! (Isaiah 30-31, Isaiah 36:6-9, 2 Kings 18:13-16, 2 Kings 19:35)

Manasseh the son of Hezekiah (probably born after Hezekiah's healing), again introduced many idol worship practises in Judah, but appears to have repented afterwards and returned to worshipping the God of Israel. Like his father Manasseh, Amon was another idolater. His name in the Hebrew means someone brought up in a skilled trade. It seems only a coincidence that his name is also the name of one of the idol gods of Egypt (Amon or Amon Ra). He faced the indignity, of being murdered by his servants.

From Josiah to the End of Judah

Amon's son Josiah was another great religious reformer. But the reforms of Josiah were not enough to stem the tide of attacks from Assyria. From him through to Jeconiah, the Southern Kingdom of Judah is under repeated attack but in the final days before the exile, we see Jeremiah the last and most important Prophet in Israel before the Exile, being saved from almost certain death by an African!

Prophet Jeremiah saved by Ebed-Melech

Jeremiah 38:7-3 tells of Ebed-Melech, a godly Cushite in the court of Zedekiah, who organised the rescue of Jeremiah from the water storage pit where he had been thrown because of his preaching. The Ethiopian Ebed-melech was one of the eunuchs in King Zedekiah's palace. He pleaded with the King to spare Jeremiah's life and helped rescue the Prophet from the pit where he had been thrown to die. Saving the prophet had a huge strategic significance for Israel.

The son of a Priest and also known as the weeping Prophet, Jeremiah's teaching brought individual relationship with God into much greater focus. His ministry was incredibly significant in preparing the people of Judah for their time in exile, when personal religion would now have to replace temple worship. Jeremiah gave them a sound survival strategy and the promise from God of an eventual return from exile to the Land of their promise. Jeremiah the Prophet is believed to have later lived in Egypt, where he eventually died and was buried in Africa. But it was Ebed-melech the African who saved the ministry of Jeremiah at a critical time!

> *Jeremiah 29:4-7 Thus says the Lord of hosts, the God of Israel, to all who were carried away captive, whom I have caused to be carried away from Jerusalem to Babylon: 5 Build houses and dwell in them; plant gardens and eat their fruit. 6 Take wives and beget sons and daughters; and take wives for your sons and give your daughters to husbands, so that they may bear sons and daughters—that you may be increased there, and not diminished. 7 And seek the peace of the city where I have caused you to be carried away captive, and pray to the Lord for it; for in its peace you will have peace.*

The Last Days of Judah

In the last days of Judah, the remaining leaders among the descendants of Abraham, Isaac and Jacob, are finally about to be taken captive from the Land of Israel Many will be removed to the Land of Babylon (originally founded by the African sons of Ham). The Jews would remain captive there until the Prince Zerubbabel and Joshua the Priest will lead the first returnees back home; roughly 70 years from when the first captive were taken. This was exactly as Jeremiah had prophesied. Another contemporary of the Prophet Jeremiah (and a fellow preacher of repentance and righteousness) was a Prophet called Zephaniah who had an Ethiopian (Cushite) father, and who wrote the book that bears his name.

In the 400 "silent" years from Malachi to Matthew, global power shifts from east to the west. We see the beginnings of the rise to world dominance by the European powers that has continued until the 20th Century when they enter what some see as a terminal decline. In the 400 "silent" years of the Bible, the global power of Babylon is succeeded first by Medo-Persia, then by Greece and then by Rome. Each of these powers will in turn rule over what today is called the Middle East. In these years, the Davidic line that carried the seed of Christ now survives by becoming poorer and almost obscure. This is perhaps God's way of hiding the lineage or bloodline of Christ from the gentile oppressors and their collaborators, during these years of turmoil. These 400 "silent years" also help set the scene so that several of the prophecies concerning Jesus as the Messiah could eventually be fulfilled in His life and ministry.

Our next focus will be the significance of and interaction with the earthly life and ministry of Jesus Christ, by the descendants of Ham, the Africans; from His birth in Bethlehem up till the death of Herod.

Chapter Ten – From Bethlehem to the Cross

The Magi of Bethlehem

The Magi is the anglicised form of the Latin/Greek a magus/Magos, derived from an ancient Persian word "Maguŝ". Zoroaster the founder of Zoroastrianism was born into a religious family or caste called the "Avestan magâunô". The reputation for esoteric wisdom and divination of these Magi, led to the name eventually being used for all forms of occult practice, and today we still have the word magician.

> ***Matthew 2:1-16*** *Now after Jesus was born in Bethlehem of Judea in the days of Herod the king, behold, wise men from the East came to Jerusalem, 2 saying, "Where is He who has been born King of the Jews? For*

we have seen His star in the East and have come to worship Him."

Who were the Magi who came to Christ in Bethlehem, and how did they know the significance of The Star? Historically the Magi originated in the Median region of ancient Persia. Beyond that, modern historians disagree as to the details, but some historians do claim that the ancient Medians were in fact Cushitic descendants of Ham. Many of the "mystery" religions of Asia had their origins in ancient Egypt and were further developed in Babylon. However as we have seen the African descendants of Ham who met Abraham and Isaac, knew and obeyed the One True God. This is further proof that the knowledge of God was originally widespread, but then began to decline.

According to Herodotus, the Magi or Magush were a tribe in Media the north of ancient Persia or what today is called Iran. Zoroaster was a member of this tribe and becomes the first priest of the religion now known by his name. Herodotus uses the term

Magi for the leaders of that religion who are described by various ancient historians as magicians and astrologers. These Magi then become the priests to the kings of Persia. The Median priests (Magi) also served in many other royal courts from India to Arabia. The Chaldean "wise men" appear to have learned from and developed the arts of the original Median Magi. The reputation of the Medo-Persian Magi for arcane knowledge attracted "clients" and "seekers after knowledge" from near and far, including students travelling from Africa. This is possibly why the Magi of Bethlehem may have come from Persia and yet appeared to be of different ethnicities.

However, there is still confusion as to the names and nationalities of the Magi who came to Bethlehem. According to Western church history, the Magi were Melchior from Medo-Persia, Caspar from India, and Balthazar from Arabia some Armenian Christians have kept this tradition from ancient times. However, there are other names given by other branches of the church and some of these names are from areas closer to the possible Persian origins of the Magi. While the Ethiopian Orthodox Church calls them Hor, Karsudan, and Basanater, the Syrian Orthodox Church calls them Larvandad, Gushnasaph, and Hormisdas; while some Armenian Christians call them Kagpha, Badadakharida and Badadilma.

We had already shown in an earlier chapter how the Bible makes it clear, that the children (descendants) of Ham (Hamitic or African people) eventually occupied lands as far as, and beyond the Tigris River, into Persia. There are also both written and archaeological finds showing ancient Persian warriors clearly as being black men with thick woolly hair. There is the possibility then that at the very least, the original Magi of Persia indeed had some Cushitic (Hamitic) ancestry which then mixed with subsequent migration into that area.

How They Knew About the Star

The Magi of Bethlehem who visited the infant Christ, came from the "East" rather than from any other direction. This categorically rules out speculation that they came from Armenia, Turkey, Europe, Africa or Arabia etc. A line drawn east from Bethlehem would instead take you through Jordan, and into present day Iran (ancient Persia), or Afghanistan, Pakistan (Greater India) and perhaps beyond. A number of ancient writers including Aurelius Prudentius Clemens, Clement of Alexandria, Cyril of Alexandria, Diodorus of Tarsus, Gaius Juvencus and John Chrysostom all agree that the Magi of Bethlehem came from Persia. It is pertinent to note that a large number of Jews were taken into exile and many of these ended up in the area known as Media. Some exiled Jews like Daniel and Esther became quite influential.

> **2 Kings 17:6** In the ninth year of Hoshea, the king of Assyria took Samaria and carried

Israel away to Assyria, and placed them in Halah and by the Habor, the River of Gozan, and **in the cities of the Medes.**

Although historians dispute which King was Darius the Mede, you will remember him from Chapters 6-11 of the Book of Daniel. Darius is brought to power by the "Medo-Persian" armies. You might recall that Darius is particularly famous for throwing Daniel into a den of lions and then apparently repenting to worship the God of Abraham when Daniel miraculously survives. There are other instances of miraculous deliverance leading to the "conversion" of the Jews' captors to the religion of the Jews.

> *Daniel 6:28 So this Daniel prospered in the reign of Darius and in the reign of Cyrus the Persian.*

> *Esther 8:17 And in every province and city, wherever the king's command and decree came, the Jews had joy and gladness, a feast and a holiday. Then many of the*

*people of the land became Jews, because
fear of the Jews fell upon them.*

The presence in Persian Media of these exiled
Jews, versed in the scriptural prophecies of the
Messiah was possibly another source of
information to the Magi who came to Bethlehem.
Perhaps that was how the Gentile Magi knew, that
a certain sign in the heavens would herald this
most momentous of events for the descendants of
Abraham. The exiled Jews and the Magi of Media
could have discussed the prophecies of Micah 5:2
and Numbers 24:17. In summary, there was no
shortage either of Jewish "converts" or leaders
from other faiths who had enough information from
the Jewish Scriptures to inspire the company of
Magi, to pay a visit to a young child in Bethlehem.
Zoroastrian Magi may have been particularly
attracted to Judaism by the structure of their own
religion and its concepts of good and evil.

Numbers 24:17 *"I see Him, but not now; I
behold Him, but not near; A Star shall come*

out of Jacob; A Scepter shall rise out of Israel, and batter the brow of Moab, and destroy all the sons of tumult.

The knowledge of the ancient Medes and Zoroastrianism could have mixed with Bible prophecies of the exiled Jews to prepare the Persian Magi for their epic journey from Persia to Bethlehem in search of the Jewish Messiah! It is almost certain that a knowledge of prophetic revelation from the Jewish Scriptures played a role in their decision to travel to Bethlehem. Their ancient astrological arts like your modern "horoscope" probably lacked any of the kind of accuracy to have reached the conclusion of the birth of the Messiah without external input. Either the Jews among them told them or perhaps they had a direct revelation from God, since He later speaks to them in a dream, warning them not to return to Herod after finding the infant Christ.

We can see that Jews used the term Magi to describe astrologers from scriptures such as

Daniel 2:2 and 10. Tertullian is the first Christian writer to call the Magi of Bethlehem "Kings". No such titles appear in the Bible. There appear to have a group of the Magi with a smaller group of leaders who spoke for the group. In some Eastern Orthodox Churches, (particularly the Syriac) the story is that there were 12 Magi. Later Christian tradition names the three leaders of the Magi of Bethlehem as Belthazar, Gaspar, and Melchior. The gifts they presented to the infant Jesus were gold, frankincense and myrrh. Whatever the number of leaders or "Kings", the needs for security and comfort mean it is more than likely, that they travelled with a retinue of guards, personal servants, apprentices and porters.

The Black Magi – Balthazar

From 12th century in Northern Europe, Balthazar was progressively believed to be Black and originally from Africa; most likely Ethiopia. From the 12th to 15th Centuries, art in Northern Europe depicting the Magi of Bethlehem showed Balthazar as a Black African. Depending which modern version you read, the Bible passage Acts 8:9, Acts 13:6 – 8, and Acts 13:8 etc. show that the term Magi was still in use in the Apostolic Era and referred pejoratively to sorcerers and magicians. These passages in the book of Acts show us that Magi were regarded as spiritual outsiders by Jews, just as shepherds were physical outsiders in many Jewish communities.

The Magi in this story were also ethnic outsiders to Israel, people whose religion and ethnicity could be traced back to the ancient Cushitic Kings of Babylon and Persia! It is interesting that these two groups (shepherds and Magi) are among the very first who recognise and acknowledge the birth of Jesus Christ, the one born King of the Jews and Saviour of the World. Since the term Magi has referred to a wide variety of belief and practice, we cannot however assume that the Magi of Bethlehem were of the same belief and practice as those mentioned in the Book of Acts.

The arrival of the Magi at Jerusalem on their way to Bethlehem, certainly caused a lot of excitement. The "wise men" were prudent enough to seek further confirmation of their intended destination from King Herod and the Jewish Scribes. Once again, it is the Scriptural prophecy of Micah 5:2 that provides corroboration for Bethlehem as their destination and the location of the One who has been born "King of the Jews". Herod officially requests that they return and tell him when this special child has been found and they then follow the star again to the conclusion of their marathon search (Matthew 2:7-10).

We may also note that the visit of the Magi seems not to take place in the stable at Bethlehem, but in a house up to two years after the birth of the Christ, and only St Mary the Virgin Mother of our Lord is recorded as present at the time. There is no mention of St Joseph the guardian or foster father at this visit, but we have no way of knowing if that absence in the text is of any significance, as we subsequently see St Joseph again in "The Flight Into Egypt".

After the Bethlehem visit, we only see the Magi again very briefly. Like the gentiles who met Abraham, the Magi know when the God of Israel speaks! Warned by God through dreams, they decide not to meet King Herod as planned. They apparently left secretly, probably because the King had people looking for them; "and returned to their own country". Herod is further enraged by their failure to meet him and redoubles his efforts to find Jesus Christ. St Joseph, St Mary and the infant Jesus are sent by God for safety into Africa. It is possible that the gifts of Gold, Frankincense and Myrrh given by the Magi at Bethlehem, came very handy in covering the expenses during the flight of the Holy Family to Egypt, of which we shall read more very shortly.

When the Saviour is Saved by Africa

> *Matthew 2:16 – 18 Then Herod, when he saw that he was deceived by the wise men, was exceedingly angry; and he sent forth and put to death all the male children who were in Bethlehem and in all its districts, from two years old and under, according to the time which he had determined from the wise men. 17 Then was fulfilled what was spoken by Jeremiah the prophet, saying:*
>
> *18 "A voice was heard in Ramah,*
>
> *Lamentation, weeping, and great mourning,*
>
> *Rachel weeping for her children,*
>
> *Refusing to be comforted,*
>
> *Because they are no more."*

The journey to Africa, was in obedience to a command from God to St Joseph, foster father to Jesus and is thought to have lasted between three and four years. Traditionally remembered as "The Flight into Egypt of the Holy Family" the sanctuary offered by Africa to the infant Jesus is still celebrated by several of the historic church denominations.

> ***Matthew 2:13-23*** *Now when they had departed, behold, an angel of the Lord appeared to Joseph in a dream, saying, "Arise, take the young Child and His mother, flee to Egypt, and stay there until I bring you word; for Herod will seek the young Child to destroy Him." 14 When he arose, he took the young Child and His mother by night and departed for Egypt, 15 and was there until the death of Herod, that it might be fulfilled which was spoken by the Lord through the prophet, saying, "Out of Egypt I called My Son" (Hosea 11:1).*

Egypt was a safe place to hide the infant Christ, as it was beyond Herod's jurisdiction. Both Egypt and Israel were still under Roman rule and linked by one of the famous Roman roads called "the way of the sea". There was an old and established Jewish community in Egypt and it is even possible that Joseph or Mary had relatives there.

The Holy Family, are said to have lived in or visited a number of places in Egypt. The Coptic (Egyptian) Orthodox Church in particular has kept the traditions of the Holy Family's time in Africa. Miracles are believed to have occurred in many of the places they stayed and though these stories may have been embellished or obscured by the passage of time, the widespread occurrence, and the depth and strength of the traditions show their possible origin on a foundation of reality. Several of the oldest churches in the world are in Egypt, built to commemorate the journey of the Holy Family, the places they stopped or lived in, and the reported miracles that occurred. Places that the Holy Family Visited or stayed in are said to include:

- Al-Maṭariyyah

- Asiut

- Assiut in Upper Egypt

- Bilbais

- Farama

- Maadi

- Samalout

- Samanoud

- Tel Basta

- Wadi El Natrun

- Zeitun in Cairo

In Cairo, other places where the Holy Family stayed are commemorated by several churches including:

- Church of the Holy Virgin (Babylon El-Darag)

- Saints Sergius and Bacchus Church (Abu Serga)

- The Chapel at Al-Maṭariyyah (St Mary's Tree)

In Eid Street/Shek El-Te'eban Street, in el-Matarya district of Cairo it is reportedly almost impossible to get bread or other bakery dough to rise and this is still attributed to a refusal of some residents of that street to give bread to the Holy Virgin Mary, 2000 years ago!

Saint Aphrodisius

In France, the man who offered shelter to the Holy Family in Africa is remembered as an Egyptian named Saint Aphrodisius who later became the Bishop of the Southern French Diocese of Béziers. Aphrodisius was originally a powerful pagan Egyptian priest. He later became a Christian and died a martyr to the Christian faith in Languedoc, Southern France, in around 65AD. Ado the Carolingian, Usuard of Paris, and Gregory of Tours, all mention this African Missionary Bishop who lived and worked in France. Gregory records that Aphrodisius died along with several Christian companions when they were attacked... by local pagans.

The Death of Herod

Eventually, Herod dies and Joseph receives the command from God to take the Holy Virgin and Jesus back to the Land of Israel. Herod probably dies between 1 – 4BC, no one is exactly sure. However, the Jewish historian Josephus records a slow, painful and terrible death for this wicked ruler. Modern doctors looking through the symptoms described by Josephus and others have supposed that Herod died of combined Chronic Kidney Disease (CKD) or chronic renal disease (CRD) combined with Fournier's Gangrene, a deadly infection which attacks the private parts and spreads, killing off the flesh which it overtakes and causing that flesh to rot while the victim is still alive. You may recall that Herod's grandson Agrippa died in similar fashion. Perhaps it "ran in the family".

Hosea 11:1 *"When Israel was a child, I loved him, and out of Egypt I called My son.*

Matthew 2:19 - 23 *Now when Herod was dead, behold, an angel of the Lord appeared in a dream to Joseph in Egypt, 20 saying, "Arise, take the young Child and His mother, and go to the land of Israel, for those who sought the young Child's life are dead." 21 Then he arose, took the young Child and His mother, and came into the land of Israel. 22 But when he heard that Archelaus was reigning over Judea instead of his father Herod, he was afraid to go there. And being warned by God in a dream, he turned aside into the region of Galilee. 23 And he came and dwelt in a city called Nazareth, that it might be fulfilled which was spoken by the prophets, "He shall be called a Nazarene."*

What does the Bible mean when it says that Jesus was to be called a Nazarene? It is worth digressing slightly from our main topic here to discover something about this meaning. Many have confused the word Nazarene with the term Nazarite. Unlike Sampson and Samuel, *Jesus was never a Nazarite*. Contrary to the Nazarite vows, Jesus drank wine and did not mind visiting graves, and even touching the dead. Rather, Jesus is called the Nazarene in reference to Isaiah 11:1. In the next chapter, we will look at some other Gentile Africans who we meet in the New Testament.

Chapter Eleven – Other Africans in the New Testament

Jesus and the Samaritan Woman

In John Chapter 4 we read about the meeting between Jesus and the woman at the well near Sychar in Samaria. Typical of the engagement of Jesus with ordinary people, this meeting happens unexpectedly on an ordinary day and changes her life (and that of many others) for ever.

Who are the Samaritans and do they have any connection to Africa? Samaritan, actually means "one who keeps of the law". Samaritanism, is very closely linked to Judaism, and Samaritans have always claimed theirs is the true religion of ancient Israel! The Jews though, felt that the Samaritans have a corrupt form of the Jewish faith. The Samaritans claimed they were descended from the remnant of the tribes of Ephraim and Manasseh (the African Houses in Israel), left behind at the time of exile. Jews believed that the Samaritans left behind at that time also became mixed ethnicly, and culturally with people from Babylon brought in by the Assyrians (2 Kings 17). We have already spoken of the Hamitic (Egyptian African) origins of Babylon and the African roots of Ephraim and Manasseh. Therefore, we can say that here was a significant meeting between Jesus and the Samaritan woman at the well, as the Saviour reaches out to those regarded by the Jews, as outside Judaism.

The "Woman at the well" is another famous female in the Bible who has been given a rather bad press. She is disqualified by her ethnicity, as a Samaritan, who have no dealing with the Jews who regarded contact with Samaritans as a source of ritual uncleanness. Jews would not have considered her a Jew, but according to her own confession, she was waiting for the Jewish Messiah to come. She is presented as highly disqualified in "human" terms, but is a good candidate for God's favour. For example she is disqualified by her gender as a woman in a very male dominated society at that time. She is no great intellectual like Nicodemus or St Paul, but is willing to act on her faith. She is of doubtful moral reputation having had a fair number of men in her life, but should probably be seen more as a victim of abuse and rejection, than the female predator she has been portrayed as.

On another day, Jesus also used the story of "the Good Samaritan" to teach His Disciples and to teach us. On the day he met the woman at the well, He *chose* to go through Samaria. He sent the Disciples to buy food locally – something most Jews would not do. We can clearly see that Jesus saw those outside the mainstream Jewish society as potentially part of the new Kingdom of God, including those from or connected to Africa... He also exposed his Disciples to teaching and field experiences that would help prepare them to go beyond the Jewish population of Israel, when the right time came.

Jesus had both a local and a global focus for His ministry and taught His disciples to have the same, but they were to go only when He considered both that they were ready, and the time was right.

> **Acts 1:8** *But you shall receive power when the Holy Spirit has come upon you; and you shall be witnesses to Me in Jerusalem, and in all Judea and Samaria, and to the end of the earth."*

It seems however that Jesus' main focus was more on the Jews in the earlier part of His Earthly Ministry (Luke 7:1-10). Later, it appears that more Gentiles were involved. An example is the healing of the Centurion's Servant found in Matthew 8:5-13. We do not know the ethnicity of the Centurion, but the Roman armies recruited from all over the Empire, including from Africa as we see in the case of St Maurice of Thebes. Jesus also "pre-instructs" his disciples to go beyond the borders of Israel and to also make disciples of all nations (Matthew 24:14, Mark 13:10).

Then we can note that in the Great Commission the Disciples are commanded to go into all the world and make disciples of all the nations (including Africa as we shall see shortly). This is in direct contrast to the perceived localism of the early mission journeys. Since we do not yet have disciples of every nation, we must assume that this process is still ongoing and will continue until Jesus returns. Matthew recorded the earlier commission to the 12 Apostles in Chapter 10:1-42, but the global commission is given in Matthew 28:16–20

> **Matthew 28:16-20** *Then the eleven disciples went away into Galilee, to the mountain which Jesus had appointed for them. 17 When they saw Him, they worshiped Him; but some doubted. 18 And Jesus came and spoke to them, saying, "All authority has been given to Me in heaven and on earth. 19 Go therefore and make disciples of all the nations, baptizing them in the name of the Father and of the Son and*

of the Holy Spirit, 20 teaching them to observe all things that I have commanded you; and lo, I am with you always, even to the end of the age." Amen.

When Jesus cleans out the money changers from the temple in Mark 11:17, He declares prophetically from Isaiah 56:7(b) that God's redemptive plan has always included all nations and all peoples. In John 10:16 we see the reference to the other sheep who need to be brought into the fold.

All these and many more scriptures speak to us of the universal call to Christ, that all may come and all may serve. Africa has been a part of this story from the very beginning. Could it be that Africa will run the "last lap of this race"? Certainly, Africans have been involved in great moves of the Gospel into Europe (with the Monastic Movement) and the Pentecostal Movement of modern times. We shall return to these questions towards the end of this book.

St Luke the Gentile Saint

St Luke the author of the third Gospel and of the Book of the Acts of the Apostles, is thought by some to have been a Gentile. In St Paul's letter to the Colossians, Luke is described as a medical doctor in addition to his missionary work with the Apostle. There are signs in his Gospel, that Luke perhaps has a wider view of the mission of Christ than the other Evangelists. He traces Jesus lineage back to Adam rather than just to Abraham. He introduces parables that show God's care for the lost, particularly in Luke Chapter 15. He was a native of Antioch (Antakia) in Syria, a city with a very interesting history, well worth a closer look.

Ancient Antioch now Antakia in modern Syria, is probably the most important city in the history of the Early Church apart from Jerusalem itself. It was called Antioch on the Orontes River to distinguish it from other cities of the same name. Formerly a Roman Colony, Antioch was also the third City in the Roman Empire after Alexandria in Egypt and

Rome itself. Some of the earliest recorded Churches, the recognition of Christianity as a religion by those of other faiths (and perhaps none) as well as Paul's first major missionary journeys, were all centred on Antioch (Acts 11:20 – 26).

Antioch had a large Jewish community. Luke was more probably not a Hellenized Jew, but a Gentile Christian from Antioch. The Apostle Peter was said to have been the first Bishop here and several of the early copies of the Gospels are also said to have been compiled here. *Some of the earliest preachers of the Gospel in Antioch came from Africa!* They may have been African Jews, from Cyrene in today's Libya (Acts 11:19) Eventually, the first major split between Christianity and Judaism would take place in Antioch (Acts 13:6).

Who were the people of Antioch, known as the Antiochenes? Although Antioch had been founded by the Greek General Selucius who served under Alexander the Great, the economic, and military potential of this location of this city, meant that it had been occupied as a settlement since at least 600 BC. Historians speculate that Antioch was founded by the Orontids, supposedly a Persian or Armenian Dynasty who succeeded the Kings of Urartu in this area. However, Scythians and the Medes whom we have already heard of were active here at the same time. We have also heard how early kings in Persia were often from Africa. *There is evidence from the ancient pagan shrines of Antioch that the town was in fact founded by Cushitic explorers from Meroe in Nubia!*

Antioch lies in the valley of the River Orontes and is one of several rivers so named. The river itself cannot be navigated, but the Orontes Valley provides a natural route that runs all the way down through today's Lebanon (the Beqaa Valley) and into Egypt! The Orontes Valley runs on into the Jordan Rift Valley and on through the Gulf of Aqaba. It then continues by linking up with the southern leg of what British explorer John Walter

Gregory called The Great Rift Valley, which finally ends in Mozambique!

The Orontes Valley has been the preferred route of armies marching to and from Egypt for centuries. It was one of the ancient highways out of Africa as the Hamitic people began their great journeys of exploration and migration that would take them to Persia, China and far beyond! Antioch was just one of the settlement they founded on that epic trek.

So was St Luke a Jew, Greek, or just someone who spoke (and wrote) that language well? There is an old tradition that he was originally a slave to a Greek family, where he began to learn his command of the Greek language. It is also interesting that Luke gives us more details of those Gentiles and particularly those of Hamitic roots than any other Gospel writer. Was St Luke trying to tell us something?

Simon of the Cross

For example, Luke tells us about the Simon the Cyrenian (Simon of Cyrene), the African who carried the Cross of Calvary (also known as Simon of the Cross).

> **Luke 23:24-26** So Pilate gave sentence that it should be as they requested. 25 And he released to them the one they requested, who for rebellion and murder had been thrown into prison; but he delivered Jesus to their will. 26 Now as they led Him away, they laid hold of a certain man, Simon a Cyrenian, who was coming from the country, and on him they laid the cross that he might bear it after Jesus.

At the Cross, once again, just as at the beginning of the life of Christ on earth, the Africans are there to support Him. When the Saviour needed to be saved as an infant, it was Africa that came to the rescue. When the Saviour stumbled on the road to Calvary, it was the African who was right there again, carrying the cross! His name was Simon and he came from Cyrene in North Africa, a place where Greeks and Africans mixed and intermarried and where there was also a significant Jewish community.

Simon of Cyrene was an African, Just like Lucius of Cyrene in Acts Chapter 13. Although we are unclear about their exact ethnicity, is St Luke deliberately introducing us to people in the Early Apostolic Church, who like him possibly have a Hamitic ancestry? In Acts Chapter 8, St Luke introduces us to the (Cushitic) Ethiopian Eunuch.

> Acts 8:26-29 Now an angel of the Lord spoke to Philip, saying, "Arise and go toward the south along the road which goes down from Jerusalem to Gaza." This is desert. 27 So he arose and went. And behold, a man of Ethiopia, a eunuch of great authority under Candace the queen of the Ethiopians, who had charge of all her treasury, and had come to Jerusalem to

worship, 28 was returning. And sitting in his chariot, he was reading Isaiah the prophet. 29 Then the Spirit said to Philip, "Go near and overtake this chariot."

We will say more about the Ethiopian Eunuch in some following pages.

The Africans Present at Pentecost

We also see that Africans were prominent in their presence on the Day of Pentecost. The Feast of Weeks (Shavuot) known to Christians as Pentecost, is an important feast in the calendar of ancient Israel. Shavuot, which commemorated the giving of the Law by God to the Jews on Mount Sinai, is the origin of the Christian feast of Pentecost. For Christians, Pentecost celebrates the sending of the Holy Spirit into the Early Apostolic Church in Acts Chapter 2. It is worth remembering that Shavuot is one of the Three Pilgrimage Festivals (Shalosh Regalim) of the Jews. These are the three times in the year when adult male Jews would make a special effort to go on pilgrimage to worship at the Temple in Jerusalem. The other two Jewish Pilgrimage Festivals are Matzos (Unleavened Bread), and Sukkot (the harvest festival). The commandments are found in the book of Exodus, Chapter 34.

Exodus 34:18-23 "The Feast of Unleavened Bread you shall keep. Seven days you shall eat unleavened bread, as I commanded you, in the appointed time of the month of Abib; for in the month of Abib you came out from Egypt. 19 "All that open the womb are Mine, and every male firstborn among your livestock, whether ox or sheep. 20 But the firstborn of a donkey you shall redeem with a lamb. And if you will not redeem him, then you shall break his neck. All the firstborn of your sons you shall redeem. "And none shall appear before Me empty-handed. 21 "Six days you shall work, but on the seventh day you shall rest; in plowing time and in harvest you shall rest.*

22 "And you shall observe the Feast of Weeks, of the firstfruits of wheat harvest, and the Feast of Ingathering at the year's end. 23 "Three times in the year all your men shall appear before the Lord, the Lord God of Israel.

So there was a major Jewish Feast in Jerusalem at the first Pentecost! God designed it so that the first Pentecostal Sermon would be heard and spread by the pilgrims. This possibly helps explain why there were the crowds of people, curious to hear what the commotion was all about, and eager to receive a fresh revelation of Scripture truth from the Lord. Then they suddenly all each heard the mainly Galilean Apostles speaking in their own languages, and the crowd included people from:

1. Arabia (the Arabian Peninsula)

2. Asia (Roman province in the western peninsula of Turkey)

3. Cappadocia (eastern Anatolia, or central Turkey)

4. Crete (largest Greek island, fifth-largest in the Mediterranean)

5. Cyrene in AFRICA (Roman province, north east Libya)

6. Egypt in AFRICA (Roman province of Egypt similar to the modern nation, except for the Sinai Peninsula)

7. Elam (Persia or southwest Iran)

8. Judea (western bank of the Jordan River, south of Jerusalem)

9. Media (Persia or northwest Iran)

10. Mesopotamia (Iraq, Kuwait, northeast Syria, southeast Turkey and parts of southwest Iran).

11. Pamphylia (south west central Anatolian peninsula, Turkey)

12. Parthia (Persia or northeast Iran)

13. Phrygia (west central Anatolian peninsula, Turkey)

14. Pontus (southern Black Sea coast or northeast Anatolia, in Turkey)

15. Rome (Capital of the Empire, still capital of Italy)

Some of these were Jewish born, others were proselytes, people who had converted to Judaism but were not originally of Jewish ethnicity. Having come to Jerusalem on Pilgrimage, many would go back to their home regions with the Good news of the Gospel. These 15 areas (above) would therefore logically be possibilities for the very earliest Christian communities, some of whom would later become organised churches.

> *Acts 2:5-13 5 And there were dwelling in Jerusalem Jews, devout men, from every nation under heaven. 6 And when this sound occurred, the multitude came together, and were confused, because everyone heard*

them speak in his own language. 7 Then they were all amazed and marveled, saying to one another, "Look, are not all these who speak Galileans? 8 And how is it that we hear, each in our own language in which we were born? 9 Parthians and Medes and Elamites, those dwelling in Mesopotamia, Judea and Cappadocia, Pontus and Asia, 10 Phrygia and Pamphylia, Egypt and the parts of Libya adjoining Cyrene, visitors from Rome, both Jews and proselytes, 11 Cretans and Arabs— we hear them speaking in our own tongues the wonderful works of God." 12 So they were all amazed and perplexed, saying to one another, "Whatever could this mean?" 13 Others mocking said, "They are full of new wine."

Christ for all the World

On the whole though, we can see that apart from His four years in Egypt, Jesus Christ did not have a great deal of interaction with Gentiles including Africans, but what few such meetings there were, could be significant. His words and actions, including the training given to the Disciples show that Jesus always intended a global mission. Perhaps He wanted to build a strong team from within Israel before they could go to the world. It is also possible that the first Christians needed to be Jews, since they (like all His early Disciples) would already be schooled in the Law of Moses and the Bible Prophecies pointing to Jesus Christ. Christians today have access to a huge body of teaching (of varying quality) built up over centuries, but at the start of the Early Church, it was not so. Teaching new generations has helped keep Jewish identity intact even in times of exile.

> *Genesis 18:19 For I have known him [Abraham], in order that he may command*

his children and his household after him, that they keep the way of the Lord, to do righteousness and justice, that the Lord may bring to Abraham what He has spoken to him."

Deuteronomy 6:1-9 "Now this is the commandment, and these are the statutes and judgments which the Lord your God has commanded to teach you, that you may observe them in the land which you are crossing over to possess, 2 that you may fear the Lord your God, to keep all His statutes and His commandments which I command you, you and your son and your grandson, all the days of your life, and that your days may be prolonged. 3 Therefore hear, O Israel, and be careful to observe it, that it may be well with you, and that you may multiply greatly as the Lord God of your fathers has promised you—'a land flowing with milk and honey.' 4 "Hear, O Israel: The Lord our God, the Lord is one! 5 You shall *love the Lord your God with all your heart, with all your soul, and with all your strength. 6 "And these words which I command you today shall be in your heart. 7 You shall teach them diligently to your children, and shall talk of them when you sit in your house, when you walk by the way, when you lie down, and when you rise up. 8 You shall bind them as a sign on your hand, and they shall be as frontlets between your eyes. 9 You shall write them on the doorposts of your house and on your gates.*

Galatians 3:24 *Therefore the law was our tutor to bring us to Christ, that we might be justified by faith.*

In those early days of Christianity, anyone who had not been schooled in the Law and the prophets, would be ill equipped to understand and teach the Gospel of Christ to Jews, or even to the Gentiles. While few were as learned as St Paul, they would all have had the basic religious education given to

Jewish children, and several Disciples of Christ had earlier been Disciples of St John the Baptist. Gradually, as the knowledge of the life and teaching of Christ and His Apostles (the Kerygma) began to spread, that began to change.

> *John 1:12 But as many as received Him, to them He gave the right to become children of God, to those who believe in His name:*

Those who believe in Jesus Christ as the Son of God and receive Him through obedience to His Commandments are now part of His Body on earth. In the glorious words of 1 John 3:2,

> *1 John 3:2 Beloved, now we are children of God; and it has not yet been revealed what we shall be, but we know that when He is revealed, we shall be like Him, for we shall see Him as He is.*

Those who speculate about the existence of a physical family, supposedly directly descended from Jesus Christ somewhere on Earth, have completely missed the point! *The believing and* obedient church is the family of Christ on earth, grafted in to the roots of Israel to the physical bloodlines that existed until Jesus Christ was born to die on the Cross of Calvary, and the spiritual lineage that God established, going back to the Patriarchs of old..

Romans 11:16-27 *For if the firstfruit is holy, the lump is also holy; and if the root is holy, so are the branches. 17 And if some of the branches were broken off, and you, being a wild olive tree, were grafted in among them, and with them became a partaker of the root and fatness of the olive tree, 18 do not boast against the branches. But if you do boast, remember that you do not support the root, but the root supports you. 19 You will say then, "Branches were broken off that I might be grafted in." 20 Well said. Because of unbelief they were broken off, and you stand by faith. Do not be* *haughty, but fear. 21 For if God did not spare the natural branches, He may not spare you either. 22 Therefore consider the goodness and severity of God: on those who fell, severity; but toward you, goodness, if you continue in His goodness. Otherwise you also will be cut off. 23 And they also, if they do not continue in unbelief, will be grafted in, for God is able to graft them in again. 24 For if you were cut out of the olive tree which is wild by nature, and were grafted contrary to nature into a cultivated olive tree, how much more will these, who are natural branches, be grafted into their own olive tree?*

25 For I do not desire, brethren, that you should be ignorant of this mystery, lest you should be wise in your own opinion, that blindness in part has happened to Israel until the

fullness of the Gentiles has come in.
26 And so all Israel will be saved, as it
is written:

"The Deliverer will come out of Zion,

And He will turn away ungodliness
from Jacob;

27 For this is My covenant with them,

When I take away their sins."

In the next chapter, we examine the role of Africa in the Early Church up to the monastic revolutions that helped the evangelisation of Europe.

Chapter Twelve – Egypt in the Early Church

Africa the Sanctuary of Christianity

In the story of Africa, Christianity and the Bible, Egypt has often been the key and after the death resurrection and ascension of Jesus Christ, Egypt would once again play a pioneering role. Africa became the hiding place of Christianity. Not only was Jesus hidden from Herod here in Africa, but Christianity itself found a home in Africa. After Jerusalem was destroyed in 70 AD, the Global headquarters of Christianity then moved to Africa. Some of the first churches outside Israel were planted in Egypt and other parts of North Africa. You will remember that the ancient Egyptians are originally Hamitic people, ethnically related to Nubians and (Cushitic) Ethiopians. Modern Egyptians show traces of European, Asiatic and other ethnicities, reflecting the history of Egypt, at the confluence of Africa and the rest of the world.

Just as people and civilisations went out from the cradle of Africa to the world, much as Israel herself had been incubated from a single family to a nation in Africa, so Christianity too would find a home in Africa, and Egypt would become the staging post for some of the most dramatic moves of the Gospel of Christ across the earth.

The Jewish Scriptures of the Mosaic Covenant were not unknown to Africa as the Ethiopian Eunuch in Acts Chapter 8,was clearly a student of the those scriptures. We cannot simply accept a hypothesis that only missionaries from Rome evangelised North Africa, because clearly there were indigenous groups of African Christians particularly, among the African Jewish Diaspora there. Some of these African Churches seem to have existed before there was even a church in Rome. We cannot also say that sub-Saharan Africa was evangelised only by European missionaries. Later in a further section of this book, we will see how so much of Africa was actually evangelised by Africans themselves.

There had been Jewish communities settled in Africa from ancient times, certainly Jews lived in Egypt in the days of Jeremiah the Prophet. In Jeremiah 44:1 we read that the Word that came to Jeremiah concerned all the Jews who dwell in the land of Egypt, who lived at Migdol, at Tahpanhes, at Noph, and in the country of Pathros. The Septuagint or Greek Old Testament was also translated in Alexandria by seventy scholars from the Jewish Community there in the 3rd Century BC.

Simeon Called Niger

In Acts Chapter 13, Luke writes of a Christian called Simeon, who is more generally called or known as Niger. This may just be because he had black hair or was a swarthy complexion, but more likely and simply, because he was Black.

The Coptic Orthodox Church

Founded by St Mark the Apostle in 61 (or 62) AD, the Coptic Orthodox Church is one of the oldest churches in the world. By Coptic tradition, St Mark was born in Cyrene in today's Libya. The history of the Coptic Orthodox Church says that St Mark founded their church in Alexandria in Egypt in 42 A.D. just eight years before he wrote the Gospel that bears his name! Eusebius and Clement both place the Apostle Mark in Alexandria at the beginnings of what is the Coptic Church today. Later writers have claimed that Mark himself was an African Jew from Cyrene. The Gospel of Mark, is believed by many Bible scholars to be the first gospel to be written down in around 50 A.D. The Gospel of Mark has also been called the Gospel of Peter because Mark is believed to have been taught and mentored by him. He is also believed by some to have travelled extensively with St Paul.

The Coptic Church (the first African church) is best known for patient faith in the face of centuries of persecution and martyrdom, and for the founding or refining and developing of Monasticism, by the Desert Fathers and Mothers. This African monastic movement, would become the catalyst for the first great and truly global growth movement in Christianity since the Apostolic Age. There has been much argument and speculation about the nature of the relationship and/or interaction between African and other European branches of monasticism. In the next few pages, will examine some of the evidence for this. What is certain is that ancient African Monasticism was a huge challenge and influence on the development of European monasticism, even where this had sometimes been original and indigenous.

In the early days of Christianity in Africa, Jews were often the first converts as we see in the account of the Day of Pentecost, there were people present in Jerusalem from Africa. With its large and thriving Jewish community, Alexandria in Egypt was therefore one of the places where the first churches in Africa were planted. Several of the Early Church Fathers were based there.

Persecution and dispersal of the Early Christians from Jerusalem began after the Martyrdom of Stephen. After the destruction of Jerusalem and the Temple in 70AD and then the Bar Kokhba War that followed, the central role of Jerusalem, Judaea and Samaria in Early Christianity was effectively ended. The Diaspora churches (outside Israel) being founded by the original Disciples and Apostles (and their own disciples) then began to take on a greater significance.

In the East of North Africa, multiple Christian groups seem to have predated the Roman Ecclesial Discipline of the Western Mediterranean, which became the Roman Catholic Church. These indigenous African churches struggled to find unity, often fragmenting into differing theologies that at worst evolved into international heresies. The indigenous churches of North Africa were regarded with suspicion by the emerging powers of the

European churches, especially by the Greco-Roman theological hegemony. Some Roman Catholic and other European churches have held a historic position that any Christian theology other than their own brand was always mistaken or even heretical. Happily that view has been slightly more nuanced by the passage of several centuries and mutual recognition (but not full communion) between churches is now considered normal.

The real Roman pioneering of the Gospel in North Africa was mainly in cities of the Western coastal plain like Carthage now a small suburb of Tunis in today's Tunisia. The hinterland, especially the mountains of North West Africa remained largely free from this early evangelisation sent out from Rome. The Eastern part of North Africa was always closer to Constantinople.

Catechetical School of Alexandria

Two main centres of the Early Church were Alexandria (Catechetical School of Alexandria), in

Egypt and Antioch now in Turkey. Antioch near modern Antakya in Turkey was once the third most important city on the entire Roman Empire and was the place where the followers of Jesus Christ were first called Christians (Acts 11:25-26). But Alexandria, established by Alexander the Great in the delta of the River Nile, would eventually become a centre of both Jewish and Christian academic excellence.

For about 300 years anybody who wanted to go to the best Bible College, went to Alexandria in Egypt. By Coptic tradition, St Mark also founded the Catechetical (Theological) School in Alexandria (Didascalium). This African school grew to be the most influential educational institution in the early Christian church! Clement of Alexandria became Dean of the School in 190 A.D. St Jerome and St Basil studied there. Other great scholars connected to this school include Didymus the Blind, Dionysius "the Great", Gregory Thaumaturgus (Gregory of Neocaesarea), Heraclas, and Origen. This African school had special wood carvings to enable blind students study there, 1500 years before the invention of braille! The Coptic Orthodox Church still runs the modern version of this ancient school which was re-established in 1893.

Origen (from Alexandria) and Tertullian who like Augustine came from the area of North Western Africa once known as the Maghrib or "Africa Minor" were among the great intellectuals and theologians of early Christianity. North Africa was also the source of several heresies as some tried to find answers to questions they found in their Christian faith. Although greatly diminished by and under continuing pressure since the Islamic invasions, North African Christianity has survived in parts of these once Christian lands, most notably in Egypt.

The Patriarch of Alexandria like those of Rome, Constantinople, Antioch, and Jerusalem has traditionally born the title of Pope. In modern practice the title is mainly used by the Bishop of Rome (head of the Roman Catholic Church), and the Primate of the Coptic Orthodox Church of Alexandria who is still known as the Pope of Alexandria and Patriarch of all Africa. There is also a Greek Orthodox Patriarch of Alexandria a circumstance reaching back to the theological controversies at the Council of Chalcedon.

The African city of Alexandria in Egypt is mentioned repeatedly in the Book of Acts where that city is often connected to various aspects of Apostolic missionary activity. For example, in Acts Chapter 18, we are introduced to an African Jew called Apollos who was born in Alexandria. Although he only knew the teaching of St John the Baptist, Apollos was busy teaching about Christianity in the Synagogues of Ephesus. Apollos would cross ministry paths with St Paul the Apostle.

> *Acts 18:24* *Now a certain Jew named Apollos, born at Alexandria, an eloquent man and mighty in the Scriptures, came to Ephesus.*

In Acts Chapter 27, it is an Alexandrian ship that takes the Apostle Paul on his journey to Rome, and his arrival in the capital of the Roman Empire is recorded in Acts Chapter 28.

> *Acts 27:5-6 And when we had sailed over the sea which is off Cilicia and Pamphylia, we came to Myra, a city of Lycia. 6 There the centurion found an Alexandrian ship sailing to Italy, and he put us on board.*

> *Acts 28:11 After three months we sailed in an Alexandrian ship whose figurehead was the Twin Brothers, which had wintered at the island.*

Three African Popes

At least three of the early Roman Catholic Popes were Africans. The first African Pope of the Roman Catholic Church was St. Victor I, who was born at Lebda in Libya and was the Bishop of Rome for around ten years from about 189 – 199. The second African Pope of the Roman Catholic Church was a Berber, St. Melchiades who was presented with the Lateran Palace by Emperor Constantine and was Pope in Rome, when Constantine declared freedom of worship for Christians. The third African Pope was St. Gelasius was born to a Roman family in Africa (possibly Carthage), and was Bishop of Rome for four years from 492 – 496.

St Antony the Great

St Antony was an African, born in Egypt. Though not the first African monastic, Antony is recognised as the greatest of the Desert Fathers, famous for his asceticism, spiritual warfare, his sharing of his faith (and learning) with others; as well as his defending the faith against heresy and encouraging the Christian Martyrs. Antony developed the monastic life, by pulling together and extending a number of existing practices, and bringing in his own innovations. St. Antony led the eremitic or hermitic (mainly isolated and secluded) monastic movement in Egypt. Saint Pachomius studied under St Antony for some time and went on to lead the Cenobitic or Coenobitic (mainly community or communal) monastic movement in Egypt. St Hillarion studied with St Antony and became a secluded but influential anchorite monk near Gaza in Israel by copying the work of the African monks.

St Athanasius

The understanding of African monasticism was mainly spread in Western Europe through Latin translations of a biography of St Antony, written by the Coptic Patriarch St Athanasius who had argued successfully against the Arian heresies at the Council of Nicea in AD 325. Later St Athanasius was exiled several times from his See in Alexandria by the supporters of Arianism. He travelled to Rome and to France (in about AD 345) where he taught extensively about the Monastic tradition already established in Egypt. The Coptic Orthodox Church which still exists today, has many churches in Britain and around the world. The African Monastic movement spread from the Coptic tradition of St Anthony in Egypt to Gaul in modern France, and from there to Ireland and to other parts of Europe.

In addition to the travelling, teaching and writing of St Athanasius, knowledge of African monasticism appears to have been passed on to St Ninian and others by St Martin of Gaul, whose mentor was St Hilary of Potiers. St Hilary was one of several Europeans who had travelled to the Middle East study to study the monastic life there. St Martin would become known as "the father of Celtic Christianity". There were many others who learned from St Antony and his desert colleagues. St Augustine and St Benedict, the "Father of the Western monastic tradition" were greatly influenced by St Antony's life and teachings. While Celtic and other European monasticism had some distinct differences, there was in fact a direct line of connection between them. Monasteries eventually became the principal centres of faith and culture for the Celtic tribes of Britain.

The Celtic Monks

As the Romans withdrew from Britain and pagan Anglo Saxons began to invade, Christianity became confined to the west of the islands and Wales, where, as in Ireland, the original Celtic inhabitants remained largely Christian. The Celtic monasteries were the strongholds of Christianity and became key to withstanding the pagans. God drew resources from there to help the re-establishing of a unique Christian spirituality in the British Islands. The years 400-600 especially, became the era of the Celtic monk-missionaries. So the African monastic Christian movement was key to the spread and preservation of Christianity in Europe!

The Monastic movement was the secret to the evangelisation of Europe that prepared European nations to spread Christianity internationally through trade, military conquest and missionary efforts. Monasticism, was the first great global movement of Christianity and it lead to the Gospel being taken "to the ends of the Earth". AFRICA WAS THE FOUDATION OF THIS GREAT MOVE OF EUROPEAN CHRISTIANITY. *The life and teaching of African Christians like St Antony was a significant factor in bringing Christianity to Northern Europe!* The African monastics also gave Christianity the "Prayer of the Hours", a system of sustaining prayer throughout each day, that is still used in many denominations, including the Coptic Orthodox Church.

The presence of "Black Madonnas" in Europe, and the venerations of a Black man St Maurice of Thebes as Patron Saint of the Holy Roman Emperors, points back to a time when Europeans saw people from Africa as leaders in and pioneers of Christianity. That remained the case from antiquity until the Slave Trade when European attitudes to their darker skinned brothers and sisters from the South began to change to justify the profit made from trading in human beings. The incorrect assumption that Africans were cursed by God "the curse of Ham" was part of the propaganda to justify the unjustifiable trade in enslaved Africans.

In the next chapter, we follow the rise and influence of the Coptic, Ethiopian and Nubian Churches.

Chapter Thirteen – The Ethiopian Orthodox Church

We have seen the enormous influence of the African monastic movement, and how the Desert Fathers and Mothers of Egypt sparked or boosted the planting of monasteries and churches right across the European region. This is a very different picture from what is taught in most schools where the standard history is that Africa was simple the "Dark Continent" until European missionaries arrived off West African Coast. Africa was also the birthplace of much of the early organised church! The Early African churches were most influential in North East Africa and the Eastern Mediterranean We have looked at the Coptic Orthodox Church. We can now look at the Ethiopian Orthodox Tewahedo Church.

The Ethiopian Royal Line

As we have seen, Ethiopians trace their Royal Line back to Cush of Genesis 2:13 making it the oldest Royal Throne still in existence today. After the relationship between Queen Makeda of Saba (Sheba) and King Solomon of Israel, the ancient dynastic throne of Cush became known in Ethiopia, as the Throne of David! Ethiopian history, claims their Solomonic Dynasty and their Throne of David were first established in Axum, by Menelik I the son of King Solomon and the Queen of Sheba; although some of the exact dates are uncertain. Today, the work of the Ethiopian Imperial House of Solomon has been carried on by the Crown Council of Ethiopia; ever since the socialist coup of 1975 forced the Crown into eventual exile.

Axum, the original capital of the kingdom of that name (which became the Ethiopian Empire), was a major regional power for more than 1,400 years. The Kebra Nagast (The Glory of the Kings) tells us that Menelik I eventually succeeds his mother on the throne and that he was given the original of the Ark of the Covenant, built by Moses to house the tablets of the Law given by God to him on Mount Sinai; as well as a retinue of Jewish priests and nobles to help him in setting up his government. *Apart from some interludes, the Ethiopian Solomonic dynasty would rule their empire for 225 generations, spanning nearly 3000 years!* However, some of the early ruling elite of the empire, appear to have wavered between the Judaism of Israel and a syncretistic mixture of this with other local religious customs.

The modern Ethiopian Imperial Family has been largely of Amharic ethnicity, but traditionally Emperors could come from other ethnic groups such as Oromo. Several of the rulers of Ethiopia have been of mixed ethnic heritage, in a nation with a history of centuries of ethnic diversity. With a long line of distinguished ancestors, many Ethiopian Emperors could lay claim to descent from King David, Solomon and some even from the Prophet Mohammed as well.

The Crown Council of Ethiopia

The Crown Council of Ethiopia is the administrative arm of the ancient Imperial Family and represents the Crown during a hiatus such as the current interregnum. Any new Emperor must be a professing, practicing Orthodox Christian in order to be enthroned; and instated only with the approval of the Crown Council. Prince Ermias Sahle Selassie Haile Selassie is the grandson of Emperor Haile Selassie I (1930-1975) who was the last of the Solomonic Dynasty to sit upon the Throne of David in modern times. Prince Ermias currently serves as the President of the Crown Council of Ethiopia according to the regulations set out in the 1955 Ethiopian Constitution. There is also a very strong and unique relationship between the Imperial House of Ethiopia and the Ethiopian Church.

The largest Oriental Orthodox Christian church in Ethiopia (and in the world) is The Ethiopian Orthodox Tewahedo Church (Ethiopian Orthodox

Church). The six Oriental Orthodox churches are all "non-Chalcedonian". For example, Tewahedo is an Ethiopian word that refers to a belief in a unique and unified nature of Christ. Like other Oriental Orthodox Churches, the Ethiopian Orthodox Church describes its belief in one indivisible nature of Christ as miaphysite (rather than monophysite), and in this they oppose the classic European dyophitic doctrine of the two natures of Christ (fully God and fully man). For these Oriental orthodox churches, the nature of Christ on Earth was totally unique and is difficult to dissect into human and Divine component parts. This has caused some historic difficulties between them and the European churches in particular. Those differences which were partly semantic and partly theological (and in some cases political as well), are now thankfully being healed.

The Ethiopian Orthodox Church has several other distinctive practices, including keeping aspects of the Jewish Kosher Laws (Kashrut) and a Saturday Sabbath in addition to Sunday Christian Worship.

Kosher practices and Sabbath observance, are among the traditions traceable to the Judaism believed to have been brought to Ethiopia by Menelik I the son of Solomon and Sheba (Saba). Early Christianity in Ethiopia on the other hand is also marked from the return of the Royal Treasurer baptised by Philip the Evangelist in Acts Chapter 8 (the Ethiopian Eunuch). However, Christianity remained a minority and elitist religion (practiced in varying forms) until Ethiopia formally adopted Christianity as the state religion, under the 4th century Axumite Kingdom led by the Emperor Ezana.

The Ethiopian Eunuch

This man is unlikely to be a Jew, since his "physical disability" would have barred him from the Temple under the Law of Moses. He is however seeking God as we meet him studying the Jewish Prophet Isaiah in his chariot, as he travels along the dusty road.

We learn that the Eunuch was a man of "great authority" under Queen Candace. There is a clue there as to who he was and where he had come from. The Queens and Queen Mothers of the ancient Kingdom of Cush (Cush was the grandson of Noah), traditionally took the Royal Title of Kandake or Kentake from which we get the modern English Candace. The Kentakes were warrior Queens who led their armies in battle. The Kingdom of Kush (now mostly in modern Sudan), was also known as Nubia and for varying periods of time was part of the Ethiopian Empire. Kings of Kush also ruled Egypt for at least a century around 700 and 600 BC. Kush continued as a Kingdom until 400AD. Nubia became a Christian nation long after Ethiopia in the 7th Century, but there were sporadic periods of Christianity there from the days of the Early Church. These early Nubian Christians were often only among the ruling elite and their highly placed officials – people like the Ethiopian Eunuch.

Like most people of Nubian ancestry, the Ethiopian Eunuch would almost certainly be a man of very dark African complexion, and was a high ranking civil servant under the Queen of the Kingdom of Kush which was at least nominally part of the Ethiopian Empire. In Ethiopia this Queen is remembered as "Hendeke" or Queen Gersamot Hendeke VII who was Queen of Ethiopia towards the end of the first half of the first century AD. It is unclear whether the names Candace and Hendeke are related. Either way, the Ethiopian Eunuch baptised by Phillip the Evangelist, was an African, employed by Ethiopian (African) Royalty.

St Frumentius and St Aedesius

Two young Syrian-Greek Christians (Frumentius and Aedesius his brother) survived a shipwreck on the coast of Eritrea. The two brothers became advisers to Emperor Ezana and are credited with his conversion and baptism. Although many of the initial Christian contacts with Ethiopia were Greek

Orthodox, St. Frumentius was later made Bishop and Patriarch of Ethiopia (known as Abune Selama) by the Coptic Patriarch St Athanasius; at the request of Emperor Ezana.

Abune Selama would organise the few scattered Christians in Ethiopia and grow the church into the beginnings of what today has become the Ethiopian Orthodox Church. The Copts traditionally appointed the Patriarch of the Ethiopian Orthodox Church which remained part of the Coptic Christianity until 1959, when it was granted autocephaly (self-governance) and its own Patriarch during the reign of Emperor Haile-Selassie I. The two churches remain closely linked.

The Coptic Orthodox Church also appointed an Archbishop for the Eritrean Orthodox Tewahedo Church in 1994 after the independence of that nation in 1993. The Eritrean Orthodox Tewahedo Church attained autocephaly in 1998.

The Nubian, Coptic and Ethiopian Churches

The old kingdom of Nubia along the River Nile (northern Sudan and southern Egypt) was invaded by the Ethiopians (Aksumites) around 350AD. As a result, three new and smaller kingdoms emerged. Nobatia in the North, Makuria in the middle and Alodia in the South. Both the Coptic Orthodox Church and the Greek Orthodox Church sent missionaries to the area. Makuria appears to have become Christian gradually in the 6th Century and chiefly among the poor, but then the King and other elites joined the new religion, wavering though in their allegiance between Constantinople and Alexandria. As Christianity seemed set to fade in northern Africa, the King of Makuria converted to Christianity and made that the official religion in his domain. By the time Islam conquered Egypt in the 7th Century, Makuria was strong enough to resist the Islamic armies and the new Moslem rulers of Egypt eventually signed a peace treaty. Makurian Kings beame the defenders of Coptic Orthodoxy, but there appears to have been no independent

Makurian church. However once trade started between the Moslem and Christian nations, Makuria gradually became filled with enough Moslem traders and others who slowly began to change the culture and the attitude to Islam.

The Ethiopian Church also experienced seasons of revival as the Islamic march across northern Africa pushed Christianity backwards there. Ethiopia was also the victim of Jihadist attacks in 1527.

One other result was perhaps that the Ethiopian Orthodox Church became even more insular and less evangelistic, perhaps failing to grasp a mandate for taking the Gospel to the surrounding nations. This may have been a great lost opportunity, but fortunately help came from outside Africa.

The Great Setback

The arrival of Islam in North Africa was a great setback for the spread of Christianity on that continent. Today we hear repeated complaints of invasion and interference by the West in "Moslem lands" and this is part of Islamist Jihadist recruitment propaganda. It seems the world has forgotten that almost all these "Moslem lands" were taken by force by Moslem Armies and the local (often Christian) population forced or coerced into accepting Islam. Only in a minority of cases was Islam spread by trade. The Western nations may not be able to say much about this since they also had great empires built by force of arms. Africans have had the misfortune to be colonised by both!

The Arab conquest of North Africa around the year 640 AD was a great setback for North African Christianity. Egypt and Ethiopia have the strongest remaining Christian communities in the north of Africa, but even here the pressure from Radical Islamists as well as from Socialist ideologues has been immense.

Clearly, there was organised Christianity in Africa long before there was in many of the places that lay claim to "ownership" of Christianity. And so what happened? Islam happened and the battle over Africa between Islam and Christianity is still continuing. Islamic terrorist against Christians existed in Africa many years before it appeared in the Western Nations. Recent reports on television have detailed the atrocities at the Westgate Shopping Mall in Kenya and by Boko Haram in Nigeria. This is a continuation of a battle that started more than 600 years ago when the Islamic armies swept into North Africa and began to move southward. More on this later.

So Africa has been key to the two greatest moves of Christian evangelisation that the world has ever known! African monasteries in Egypt were the key to the early evangelisation of Europe. From here the movement to plant monasteries spread to Syria and to Europe, and the monks they produced became the evangelists of Europe and beyond. Without the African monasteries and their monks Christianity would not have spread so rapidly. The first monasteries started in Africa, in the Egyptian desert. Whether you're talking about the eremitic, the hermitic, monastic life of St Anthony, the Father of monks or you are talking about the Cenobitic or the communal type of monastic life when we talk about St Procopius, it starts in Africa. It spreads to Syria, then to Gaul and then throughout Europe.

It is said that the Christian monks from Egypt travelled as far as the west of Ireland preaching and spreading the gospel. If you go to the western coast of Ireland to some of the oldest churches there, you will find inscriptions that appear to be in the Coptic language of Egypt. And so the very first expansion or explosion of Christianity in the world started from Africa. The second great move of the Gospel from Africa and her descendants is the Pentecostal revival now sweeping the world. We shall say more about that later.

This is very different from the view that Africa lay in total darkness until Europeans brought them the light of the Gospel of Christ. That may have been true in some parts of Africa, but even there, evangelisation rarely truly succeeded until it was taken over by the Africans themselves, and their brothers and sisters who had returned from the Americas and the Caribbean. In the next chapter, we look at the arrival of Islam in Africa.

Chapter Fourteen –Islam Comes to Africa

Early Islamic Contacts

Africa was the first to welcome the Hebrews who became a nation called Israel in Egypt. Alexandria in Egypt was the first real African home of Christianity when Jerusalem was destroyed by the Roman army. Ethiopia in Africa was also the first refuge of the Moslems who were then a persecuted minority in Arabia.

Christian Ethiopian rulers gave safe refuge to the Prophet Mohammed's Son-in-Law and a group of other Moslems. The Prophet Mohammed sent twenty three of his followers (including his son-in-law) to Ethiopia for safety in 614AD. They and others who joined them, were given safe sanctuary by the Christian Ethiopian Emperor Armah, and they stayed with him for fourteen years. Emperor

Armah repeatedly refused to hand these Moslem refugees over to the pagan Arabians, who demanded them from him. This act of Christian chivalry earned Emperor Armah the highest commendation from the Prophet Mohammed who decreed that Ethiopia should be spared from Jihad and Mohammed mourned openly when his friend, Armah the Christian Emperor died.

However, the heavy handed economic and religious policies of the Christian Ethiopian Emperor Zara Yaqob combined to create an opportunity for an Islamic uprising in Ethiopia led by Ahmad ibn Ibrihim al-Ghazi. He was financed and armed by the Ottomans and this gave him initial success until the Portuguese Church and Royal Court supplied the Ethiopian side. The change, (what some may call a hardening) in the attitude, (of previous tolerance) of Ethiopian leadership towards the different peoples in the Empire, and even towards surrounding nations, is traceable to a moment in history, and stemmed from a sense of betrayal from the attack on them; by their Islamic subjects.

Subsequent Islamic leaders have disobeyed the instruction of the Prophet Mohamed to leave Ethiopia as a Christian nation. In recent years, funding from the Gulf to Moslem groups in Ethiopia has caused the church much problems there.

Ethiopian historians have also disputed the more recent claims that Emperor Armah converted to Islam, pointing out that the Imperial Family remained Christian and Emperor Lij Iyasu (Eyasu V) lost his ascent to the throne in 1917 because of suspicions about his closeness to Islam. There have also been claims by some writers that another Ethiopian Emperor called Najashi was a Moslem, but that name is not found in the official lists of past Ethiopian rulers. However, the late Empress Menen, wife of the late Emperor Haile Selassie, was a direct descendant of the Prophet Mohammed! There are therefore a number of Christians Princes and Princesses from Ethiopia who can also claim to have descent from Mohammed, the Prophet of Islam.

The Islamic Invasion of Africa

All of Christian North Africa was overrun by the armies of Islam within fifty years. Egypt was conquered in 641AD, Libya in 645AD, Tunisia in 47AD, Algeria in 680AD, and Morocco in 690AD. In 711, fighting on one side of the European wars in Spain and Portugal, Moslem armies made their first crossing of the Strait of Gibraltar into Europe. In the 9th Century the first Moslem Sultans are appointed in the Horn of Africa. In the 10th Century we see the rise of the Almoravids in the area of Senegal, and they begin to attract local rulers into their ranks. However it took much longer for Islam to spread into the interior of Africa.

The first widespread jihad in West Africa, (which failed to make much impact) was reportedly in Mauritania in the 17th century. Later Jihads in the 19th century were much more effective at changing society and in their aim of "purifying" the early Islam practices in Africa. One of the most successful of these Jihads was led by Usman dan Fodio from 1802 in Northern Nigeria, and centred the religious, legal and commercial power in the hands of Fulani Emirs who replace the former Hausa Sultans. A number of other Jihads followed, copying dan Fodio, mainly in the Senegambia.

The Kanem-Bornu Empire became Moslem in the 11th Century, the Ouaddai Empire and the Kano Kingdom in the 16th Century, and the Sokoto Caliphate was established in the 19th Century. The Mali Empire became officially Moslem in 1324 and its successor the Mande Songhay Empire which lasted from the 1430s to about 1591 was also officially Moslem. The Songhai Empire, between the 15th and 16th centuries was one of the largest African Islamic Empires and left behind the legacy of great institutions, including the Great Mosque of Jenne, still the world's largest earthworks building

In contrast to North and parts of Western Africa, the Eastern Coast did not suffer sustained military conquest by Islamic armies. Here the progress was slower, and more based on commercial and other factors as trade between the Moslem world and people of the Pacific Rim increased. The Zanzibar Sultanate was established in 1856 and from there Islam penetrated into Congo and as far as Malawi. Islamic trade routes down the East African Coast were therefore key to the spread of the new religion which reached Mozambique although the numbers of converts or adherents were few.

So Islam was not only spread by conquest in Africa. Orderly administration won many over, including several Berber tribes in North Africa. As Moslem traders spread out over the continent of Africa, they stablished new networks through intermarriage, and new business links; a process that still continues today. Berbers tribes also revolted successfully for about five years against Islamic rule.

New lines of authority and leadership were formed based on Islamic models and principles. African traditional religion was not always removed, in some areas it was absorbed into new interpretations of Islam that allowed local culture to continue. Some Africans were also naturally attracted to Islam's spiritual message, others perhaps to the possibility of new status and power. Islamic learning probably fascinated some of those of a more scholarly persuasion. Literacy was also an asset in developing trade.

In many other parts of Africa, many people continued to mix their African traditional beliefs with the new Islam. This is still the case in many parts of Africa today and is mirrored by syncretistic practise in other religions as in some of the African Instituted Churches (AICs).

The development of Islam in many African communities may have lessons for other parts of the world. Early on groups of Moslems lived in isolated groups of traders and other business travellers, within a host community. Next members of the elite of the host community would be attracted to the new religion, mixing ideas from Islam with their own spirituality. In the final phase there would be a push from within the Moslem community for a purification of the religious practice and the adoption of Sharia.

The spread of Islam was also strengthened by founding local Sufi Moslem brotherhoods each led by their own Sheik. Sufis use memorisation and chanting of Koranic verses and the "names of God" combined with physical movements including dance to induce stated of heightened consciousness. Usman dan Fodio who led the Fulani Jihad of 1804–1808 from Sokoto, in present-day Nigeria and Cameroon, had reportedly once belonged to the Qadiri branch of Sufism himself.

Hausa, Fulani and Kanuri

We shall be using Northern Nigeria, the home of Boko Haram as a case study as we examine the challenges that Islam poses for the average Christian in parts of Africa. While there are many ethnic minorities across the north of Nigeria, the story of Islam in Nigeria needs to be told primarily in the context of three groups of people, The Hausa (in the North centre), the Fulani (to the North west) and the Kanuri (to the North east). There are other significant groupings of Moslems in Nigeria, particularly among the Yoruba further south, but these first three will help form the broad basis of our study. In studying conflict in the areas covered by the former European empires, it is always useful to remember that the people you study spill over the national boundaries created by European colonisers.

The Hausa have some ethnic diversity within a cultural and linguistic homogeneity, mainly found in Nigeria and Niger, but also in Cameroon, Chad,

Ivory Coast (Côte d'Ivoire), Gabon, Ghana, Sudan and Togo. The Fulani (Fulah) people are more ethnically and culturally homogenous, but even more widely dispersed. Fulfulde is their common language. They were traditionally nomads, some of whom settled in various places, but many remain nomadic cattle herders. They are found right across West Africa, as far north as Sudan and Egypt and also in parts of Central Africa. The Kanuri or Yerwa people are diverse ethnically, but more localised to the area around Lake Chad. The core Kanuri generally trace their origins to the rulers of ancient Kingdoms of Kanem and Bornu. Thus they often still see themselves as "above" the other Kanuri (and other groups) living in the Lake Chad area. There has been a historic rivalry among the Hausa, Fulani and Kanuri as to who should be acknowledged as the "true" custodians of Islam in Northern Nigeria and beyond.

The ruling lineage of the Kanuri of North East Nigeria claim that they are descended from King Sayf ibn Dhī Yazan of Yemen, from a Prince Sef who arrived in Kanem in the 9th Century. The defeat of Ethiopian (Aksumite) rule over Yemen and Southern Arabia is attributed to King Sayf ibn Dhī Yazan of Yemen, with the help of a Persian army (from modern Iran).

As happened in Sokoto (and elsewhere in the former Empires) colonial authorities deposed and replaced local African rulers at their will, or sided with and resourced those who were more ready to work for them. On a few occasions this meant that cruel tyrants were removed from oppressing their people. Generally it simply meant that colonial commercial and political interests were protected. Some may argue that similar things are still happening. Today the Kanuri are also the core of the Boko Haram fighters, affiliated to ISIS, but Boko Haram do have some Hausa, Fulani (and others) working with them.

The next chapter traces the efforts to bring Christianity to sub-Saharan Africa by sea.

Chapter Fifteen –Christianity comes by Sea

The evangelisation of sub-Saharan Africa had been interrupted by the arrival of Islam in the 7th Century, which spread into the Sudan and across the Sahel regions including the Christian enclaves in today's South Sudan. By the 16th Century, the North of Africa was predominantly Moslem, with only a few really significant Christian minorities for example in Egypt. Islam was also spreading by trade and conquest down the east coast of the continent. The large scale trade in enslaved Africans was originally started by the Islamic invaders and only later copied (and surpassed) by Christian Europe.

Seaborne Missions for Evangelisation

However the 16th Century also saw the beginnings of a European-led seaborne evangelisation of

West and Central Africa which effectively bypassed the largely Moslem North and went directly to the heartlands of Africa. Unfortunately this coastal missionary effort was extremely slow, hampered by lack of volunteers, disease, poor communications and by the trade in slaves which gave Europeans a bad reputation among the Africans. We shall look at the trade in enslaved Africans in more detail in another chapter.

Early pioneers in this seaborne evangelisation of Africa were the Portuguese. The Carthaginian's and Phoenicians had sailed these seas and even circumnavigated Africa centuries before, but the Portuguese are the first of the European Empires to bring the Christian message of the Gospel round the coast of West Africa. The Portuguese first set up missions in the Cape Verde Islands, São Tomé and Príncipe (Saint Thomas and Prince's Islands) and a mission to Warri in present day Nigeria. The Highlight of early Portuguese missionary success was the conversion of the Kingdom of Congo under Nzinga Cuvu (the Mani Congo) and Alfonso 1 his son.

Christian African Rulers

The Mani (Paramount King) of Congo Nzinga a Nkuwu (João I of Kongo) ruled this Central African Kingdom from 1470 to 1506. He converted to Christianity and was baptised 1491. He married Queen Nzinga a Nlaza and they had a son Nzinga Mbemba who was baptised as Alfonso 1 and ruled from 1507 -1543. King Alfonso 1 was greatly disturbed by the slave trading of the Portuguese Christians among his people and this contributed to the failure of the mission. This clash between the Christian preaching of Europeans and their trade in enslaved Africans was to be the downfall of many early missionary efforts into Sub-Saharan Africa.

However, under João I and Alfonso 1, Christianity eventually became part of the daily life and culture among rulers in the Kingdom, with many of the elite visiting Europe and even receiving theological training. Some of the African Christian practices such as the Congo version of Pinkster would be carried across the dreaded Middle Passage by enslaved Africans and revived in North America. This cultural and religious link also proves that just as some of the slaves in the Americas and the Caribbean were Moslems before enslavement, some were definitely also African Christians before enslavement and possibly some of those enslaved were African Jews.

Progress and Setbacks

The initial missionary efforts of the Portuguese were boosted by involvement and cooperation with other nations, but the Congo mission was eventually destroyed by a combination of civil war and external military attack. Sickness, especially malaria, long support and communication lines were a constant problem. Whenever the political or military fortunes of the sponsoring European power declined, as happened with Portugal, the fortunes of their missionaries in Africa also suffered. However, the greatest enemy of the early missionary efforts by Europeans in sub-Saharan Africa was the Slave Trade itself. Where European missionaries collaborated with and even participated in the Slave Trade; that caused a very negative impression among the same African that they sought to convert to Christianity. However when the missionaries resisted the Slave Trade, they could often be swept aside by the powerful interests who were already making huge fortunes from the dastardly business of buying and selling fellow human beings.

Portugal would however remain one of the pioneers of sub-Saharan Christian evangelisation, until the decline of their maritime empire (based on slaves and spices). They lost to the increasing influence of Dutch, English and French in what became the peak of the trade in enslaved Africans. As noted, the capture, buying and selling of people as slaves did little to recommend Christianity to the Africans.

The estimated number of Africans shipped across the Atlantic during the Slave Trade could be as high as twelve million. But less than eleven million would have arrived due to the number of deaths on the Middle Passage. Breeding programs imposed on the enslaved Africans in then British North America, meant that although fewer slaves were landed there than in South America and the Caribbean, the numbers in North America would become the largest, making up more than a third of the total population in the Southern States of what would become the USA, but less than fifteen percent of the entire population.

Although Portugal had pioneered the trade in Africans, with the blessing of the Roman Catholic Pope, Britain would rival and even eclipse Portugal in stripping Africa of the cream of her population. However, most Portuguese slaves went to South America or the Caribbean, while most British slaves went to North America and the Caribbean. At the height of the trade in enslaved Africans, Britain was one of the greatest of the participants in this evil commerce. Later, Britain would also become the major opponent of slavery, but other forms of exploitation of the human resources of the empires would persist for many years.

The Berlin Conference of 1884–85

The Berlin Conference of 1884–85, (the Congo Conference) apart from initiating the political and economic scramble for Africa, also marked the beginning of a new wave of missionary activity by Europeans across the continent. The second phase of the evangelisation of sub-Saharan Africa would have to wait for the ending of slavery through the combination of changing economics, the slave uprisings and the Abolition movement.

The next chapter looks at slavery, wars, disease and corruption in Africa.

Chapter Sixteen – Retribution for Africa's Contribution

The Price Africa Has Paid

Why then has Africa suffered from so many cycles of invasion, civil wars, famine, disease, exploitation, subjugation and destabilisation? Could it be that this is the price Africa has paid for defending and protecting the lineage of Christ? Could this be the price Africa has paid for giving the West organised monasticism? WE BELIEVE THE ANSWER IS YES. Africa's problems go deeper than poor governance and corruption. Some of these problems are practical, but others are deeply philosophical and even spiritual. We can view the suffering of Africa as a "counter attack". Many of these and other problems are the retribution for Africa's contribution to the global plans of God and the Gospel! Domination of the

African land mass, it's human and other natural resources; or at least control of certain key areas of these has always been key to economic development of nations outside Africa and to their ability to grow and maintain global political power. The battle over Africa continues into our own generation as we shall see later in this book.

Africa has suffered long and suffers still, but two episodes in her history stand out casting a long shadow into the present. Both are related. The first is the Islamic invasion that halted the spread of the ancient indigenous African Christianity that was spreading from Egypt and Ethiopia southward. Certainly, the Islamic nations (or areas of nations) on the African Continent have not shown much propensity for physical, economic and human development. Rather, Islamic Africa has tended to lower levels of development. The second related disaster that hit Africa was the growth of the international organised trade in enslaved Africans.

The Era of Slavery

Another major price paid by Africa for her role as custodian and caretaker of the lineage of Christ has been the scourge of slavery. Between 1700 and 1780 slavery exports from Africa had more than doubled to 80,000 and would soon make even that figure seem miniscule. Apart from West Africa, the major outlet of enslaved Africans to the Americas was from the area of Angola. On average, fifteen percent (often more) of the human cargo was lost at sea during the dreaded "Middle Passage".

So much blood was shed during this season of Africa's history that the echoes of the collective traumatising of a continent and her people, remain with us still, in many different ways. We explore this "collective post-traumatic stress" and try to examine some practical as well as spiritual solutions in this book.

Islamic Slave Traders

Although there were Jews involved in trading slaves in Europe and the Mediterranean, it was Moslem slave traders who had greater impact on Africa. Slave trading among the Islamic nations predated Islam, but appears to be condoned and (some would say) even promoted by that religion, at least in certain interpretations of it. During the Medieval period, slaves were bought and sold into the Moslem world and Byzantine (or Eastern Roman Empire), from Southern, Central and Eastern Europe. Many of these were captives from inter-tribal and other wars in Europe. The majority of these slaves were European, until the Islamic nations began their conquest of Sub–Saharan Africa, and showed Europe another source of cheaper and often stronger slaves. However the enslavement of Africans was characterised by periodic revolts, even in areas where severe and systematic oppression was used against them. France and Britain would later find this out to their cost in the Caribbean.

Islamic slave traders had brought many Bantu and other African slaves into the Mesopotamian region and what today is called the "Middle East" and also to the Indian sub-Continent. A series of uprisings between 869–883AD; by more than 500,000 enslaved Africans and poorer citizens (known as the Zanji rebellion) in today's Iraq, greatly disrupted the Islamic slave trade. The resulting turmoil also affected the political stability in the region and eventually led to a change of Government in Egypt.

The practice of Islamic fighters taking Christian women and girls captive has a long history, and did not start with ISIS and Boko Haram. Mainly Moslem Barbary Pirates from North Africa regularly raided European coastal towns and cities between 11th to the 19th century, for Christian slaves. In 1189, Almohad caliph Yaqub al-Mansur raided Lisbon in Portugal and captured 3,000 women and children. These Christian women and girls would then be sold at slave markets in North Africa and the Middle East. Islamic raiders also demanded huge ransoms to return Christian captives to their home countries. Islamic raiders also captured many Asians and sold them into slavery.

The Roman Catholic Church attempted to prohibit slavery in Europe, but could only effectively ban the exporting of Christians into slavery by other Christians. Later, the Popes would grant European Christian Kings and Queens the "right" to trade Moslem, pagan or other non-Christians as slaves, with the notable exception of Native Americans. In Britain, slavery remained legal with large markets at Chester and Bristol, supplied by Danes, Welsh and Mercian raiders, until 1102, when slavery became illegal in England. That law would not stop the English from becoming very active participants in the Trans-Atlantic trade in enslaved Africans.

All the early Islamic empires in Africa such as Ghana, Mali and Songhai were heavily dependent on slavery and slave trading and sometimes had between a third and half of their populations, made up of slaves.

Up to 18 million people were enslaved by the Islamic raiders and traders between 650 and 1900 and these included people from several other regions including Africa. For the last one hundred and fifty years of that period, the focus of Islamic slavery had shifted to Africa and the majority of the slaves were now definitely Africans. By now, Christian European and Islamic slavers were in direct competition over the enslaved Africans.

The single greatest conduit for enslaved Africans into the Islamic Middle East, was the Sultanate of Oman which took control of the strategic islands of Zanzibar in 1698. From here, the Sultans controlled the Great Lakes region and sent other raiding parties far into Central Africa, as far as the Congo. First in 1822 and then finally in 1873 the Sultan of Zanzibar was forced by the British Navy to end the slave trade on those islands. Slavery unfortunately continued on the mainland of Tanzania until it became a British colony, taken from Germany after the First World War.

Kings of the African Slave Trade

The great empires of coastal West Africa also grew powerful during and through the trans-Atlantic trade in enslaved Africans. There was some coercion by European navies, but there were also and perhaps more often, willing participants. It was an opportunity for example to get rid of opponents, to war on and plunder rival kingdoms and even to get rid of neighbours and take their lands etc. There was no secret as to the fate of those sold into the slave ships, and yet the trade went on...

This was a time of fierce inter-tribal wars and great internal turmoil for Africa, and you do not have to scratch far beneath the surface of modern Africa to find that the legacies of those terrible years are still fresh in the distrust between certain tribes and ethnicities for example. The trade in enslaved Africans resulted in shifts in demographics, gender balance, changes to economies and sometimes sudden and large drops in population. The effect of all these is yet to be quantified and perhaps never will be.

There is some evidence that indigenous slavery in Africa before the arrival of first Islamic and then European industrialised slavery was a different practice. Slaves in ancient Africa were almost part of the family and could rise to very senior positions in society. It seems that as bad as slavery in ancient Africa was, the arrival of non-African slave traders completely changed the nature of slavery in Africa for the worse. Armies of slaves were often used to raid for more slaves and the vicious cycle continued. As in European tribes that practiced human sacrifice (but at a much larger scale) slaves in Africa were often and almost always the victims chosen for sacrifice. The position of women was also made much worse than before and polygamy and concubinage became exaggerated by the availability of large numbers of vulnerable African women captured as slaves. People were also pledged to work as slaves to pay off a debt in what has been called Pawnship or debt-bondage.

There were also large numbers of slaves in Christian Ethiopia and her imperial armies brought back captives from battles who were later sold as slaves, often to Islamic traders working with the Sultanates to the North and East.

Generally, we can say that slavery was tolerated by European and other Christian powers as long as it was convenient politically and profitable commercially, until pressure from abolitionists, growing slave revolts and the innovative machinery of the Industrial Revolution made abolition painfully inevitable. There is also an argument that the profits from the Slave Trade helped make the Industrial Revolution possible. The terms under which the Slave Trade ended were and still are controversial. In Britain for example, huge compensation was paid to the companies trading in slaves, as a condition for closing down the trade. The freed slaves in the Americas and the Caribbean got nothing, and were to endure discrimination and oppression for many generations, a tribulation that echoes down into our own day. Emancipation changed slavery in Africa, but did not eliminate it. Across Africa, the new emancipation laws were often applied inconsistently and even selectively, with colonial and other authorities protecting African slave owners, rather than the newly (supposed free) slaves. The European-led trade in enslaved Africans officially ended but the relationship with Africa did not change. For the European powers and for many other nations, Africa would remain a source for raw materials and a market for exports.

Racism from non-Africans and feelings of worthlessness among some Africans themselves as well as class distinctions in Africa stemming from distortions of society from slavery times are some of the legacies of this deadly history. Prior to the trade in Africans, Europeans saw them as noble and advanced in many important areas of civilisation. All that would change with the deliberate dehumanising of the African, in order to justify buying and selling the children of Africa.

Diseases in Africa

Another seeming repercussion for Africa's support for the plans of God, has been a continual ravaging by deadly diseases. Over centuries, the Continent of Africa has become known as the "home" of several deadly diseases. This is another legacy that Africans have had to live with and overcome. These diseases are found elsewhere but several have particularly made their "home" in Africa for a number of reasons including the basic problem of poor governance. Here is a list that does not claim to be complete.

Amebiasis	Leishmaniasis
Cholera	Lymphatic
Dengue Fever	Malaria
Diarrhoea	Malnutrition
Ebola	Onchocerciasis
Filariasis	Polio
Giardiasis	Schistosomiasis

Guinea-Worm	Sickle Cell
Hepatitis	Syphilis
HIV/AIDS	Trypanosomiasis
Hookworm	Tuberculosis
Hypertension	Typhoid
Jaundice	Yellow Fever

For example, more than 4 million people in Africa die each year from infections of the lower respiratory tract such as pneumonia, tuberculosis, whooping cough, Legionnaire's disease, and other diseases of the larynx, trachea, bronchi, bronchioles and the lungs. These types of diseases are spread by simply exhaling breath, or by coughing, sneezing or laughing, and children are the major victims. Poverty, crowed slums and HIV AIDS also greatly increase the risk of developing LRTIs. The lack of adequate diagnosis and treatment, including the availability of fake drugs means that death tolls are much higher than they otherwise would be. Poor planning, incessant wars, including terrorism, corruption and capital flight aided by the Western banking system make the prioritising of resources to child medical care almost impossible. Meanwhile the MDG Goal number 4 was to reduce child mortality.

Although access to anti-retroviral drugs is improving, HIV-AIDS remains a major problem on the continent as are a number of other deadly diseases like Malaria and Diarrhoea. While poverty remains a contributor to disease, in a vicious cycle, disease is also a contributor to poverty, through erosion of the human resources of the continent.

The link between improving healthcare and accelerated socioeconomic development seems to have eluded most African leaders. Poor work conditions also contribute to increasing numbers of Africa healthcare workers migrating to Europe the Middle East or the USA in search of better jobs. *The elite of the African nations then go to foreign hospitals, to be treated by the same doctors and nurses who come from the same nations as them!* Foreign investors also seem to have missed the potential of investments in African healthcare. Political instability, violence and war have also degraded healthcare capacity, and greatly increased exposure to poverty and disease.

Wars in Africa

War is not new to Africa, any more than to other regions of the world. What is remarkable is that after WWII, other continents increasingly experienced shorter wars and longer peace. Africa during and immediately after the Cold War, seemed conversely to be moving towards increasing frequency of conflicts, although often confined within nations or regions. During the Cold War, a number of proxy conflicts linked to geopolitical and economic interests of the "Super Powers" and their satellites raged across Africa.

The trade in enslaved Africans exacerbated inter-ethnic, tribal and other tensions and external powers armed different kingdoms and factions to facilitate the export of the human resources. The major slave hunting wars ended with the closing down of the European, American and Caribbean markets, with the gradual abolition of the trade in enslaved Africans. This model of ending supply by closing down the market, may have lessons for the battle to stem the flow of narcotics into Western Europe and America. However the 20th Century wars in Africa have also been largely driven by the need for external "businesses" to gain access to local raw materials, whether you speak of the timber and diamond wars of Sierra Leone and Liberia, or those giving opportunities for other commodities to be extracted from the Republic of Congo (Congo Brazzaville) and the Democratic Republic of the Congo (Congo Kinshasha, Former Zaire) etc.

Between 1990 and 2007 the majority of deaths in conflict were in Africa. From then, the numbers began to decline, but with the continuing fighting in the Democratic Republic of Congo (DRC), the Central African Republic, Angola and the activities of Boko Haram, AQIM and ISIS in Libya the numbers of conflict deaths in Africa are rising steeply again.

2014 was a year filled with bad news for Africa from Boko Haram to Ebola, the continent continued in the trend to the ravages of conflict and disease, resulting in thousands of deaths. Africa remains divided along ethnic, tribal and religious lines which cross over the often artificial international boundaries imposed by European colonisers. Consequently, political, economic and military problems in Africa also often have these same divisions and therefore easily spread within and beyond the modern state boundary. This miss-management of Africa by "remote control" reached its zenith under military and other dictatorships during and just after the Cold War, and still continues today. Africa is the youngest continent and her youth are often the poorly trained and exploited urban masses, who can too easily be enticed into becoming armed combatants in African conflicts, including radical militant Islamism;

and sadly, *the young generation of Africans are the greatest losers in the continuing exploitation of their continent.*

Bad Beginnings

The European Empires were chronically short of human resources and also struggled to cope with the transitions to independence by the colonies. Most of the handovers were done in a political rush, without time to enculturate the values of the proposed new European-style democracy, or subjection of the military forces to the civilian authorities of the new nation. The wider society of the new country was also often ill prepared for the new democratic engagement, which was usually the preserve of the small handful of Western educated elite, who stepped into the mansions and privileges of the departing colonisers. However the emerging elite often had mixed feelings towards the West. The economies of the emerging states had been geared to serve the resource needs of the Colonisers and would struggle to become economically independent, with subsequent generations of African leaders tending to follow the old formulae of alliances with foreign business and politicians in selling off the resources of African nations.

Although there have been many signs of welcome growth of indigenous businesses in several sectors across Africa, it sometimes appears that the populations of many African nations still prefer to see foreign business leaders taking their national resources. Many Africans often seem to become resentful of fellow Africans who show signs of business success, even where these have been legitimately earned. There has been an apparent backlash from the old western multi-national hegemonists and their "local agents". African entrepreneurs who back a political party that loses an election may also face ruin in the "vendetta" that follows.

The response of the USA and European nations to crises across Africa, while commendable in the Ebola outbreak, remains selective. The trend has been to turn a "blind eye" while their multi nationals partner with African political elites to plunder the resources of Africa. Although that is gradually changing, the USA and Europe usually wait until their citizens or immediate economic interests are directly threatened, or until African politicians who are amenable to their interests need their support. The short-termism of this focus on economic and political hegemony for extraction of African resources by the West (and latterly China), has often left African nations even more unstable, and therefore unable to provide the longer term partnership that would have been a greater benefit to all.

According to a 2011 UNDP report almost all the countries ranked bottom on the Human Development Index are African and this is often due to political, economic and military crises. Writing in 2014, Swiss researchers Berman *et al*, from the Graduate Institute of International and Development Studies and CEPR, show how the rise in international commodity prices can often mean a corresponding rise in conflict in Africa. Between 1997 and 2010, their research linked 65% of the violence in Africa to rising commodity prices caused largely by the rising demand from China. Other researchers have shown how falling commodity prices can also cause rises in violence on the continent and that African communities and their people are also treated as commodities by combatants. As always, these problems are also opportunities for the churches to help provide solutions

The nations created by the colonisers of Africa often had inherent ethnic and religious divisions with multiple potentials for later conflict, helping make them vulnerable to economic and political weakness. These nations were also created without much thought to their strategic military defence. Missionaries from Europe had also expended great efforts and lost many lives in starting the spread of Christianity through sub-Saharan Africa, but the inherent instability of many of the nations created by Europe in Africa has had implications for Christianity; and for the relations with other faiths like Islam. The churches that were planted from Europe into Africa were also often as divided as the churches in Europe that planted them. European Christian Missionaries often brought division and denominationalism along with the Christianity they brought to Africa. The challenges confronting the continent of Africa now require churches to put aside denomination and other differences and work together for the people of Africa.

In the 20th Century the rise of the cities almost as modern city states with their own economies, and international connections have combined with the rise of social media to almost "bypass" the notion of the nation state, and give people a new sense of identity based on new networks of connections and allegiances. Encryption and the "dark web" enhance networks of crime and terror on a global scale. These have had impacts in economics, religion, politics and in the new forms of terrorism and organised crime. The economic, political and social conditions in which many African nations came to independence contained the seeds of tragedy, including civil war. All over Africa and across the world, the artificial borders of colonialism are also crumbling or simply being ignored, as we witness what may be the last days of disintegration of the old European Empires. The nations they tried to create to suit their economic and political interests around the world are in turmoil and increasingly, the borders and institutions of those nations are crumbling. That is part of the secret of the success of Boko Haram and ISIS and others who operate as if the old colonial boundaries never existed. These problems look set to continue for some time to come.

Europe became the "home" of Christianity after the fall of North Africa to Islam. But in recent years, Europe has suffered from uncertainty of Christian Doctrine, falling church attendance and a transition from Christendom, through multi-culturalism, to "multi-faithism". This gradual trend has also affected politics and other areas of life. One of the great strategic errors of Christian Europe was to align with Middle Eastern nations due a reliance on oil without realising the significance of the assets in sub-Saharan Africa. European nations have allowed themselves to be cut off from a secure land route into Africa from the Mediterranean.

Dependence on Oil

The struggle by the West to control Middle Eastern oil at all costs has helped the increasing relationship between the West and Islam. Coinciding with a time of reduced interest in Christianity and a rise in attacks by radical Islamists, the West has often found itself caught between "a rock and a hard place" in trying to manage the relationship with the Middle Eastern oil producers. Relationships with the Islamic nations need to be more balanced and reciprocal. The west also needs to stop turning "a blind eye" to the plight of minorities and other human rights issues in the Moslem nations they call their allies. The selective foreign policy and human rights stance of Western Governments is eroding confidence in leadership among ordinary people, especially the young, and may even be contributing to radicalisation.

Dependence on oil has meant that huge levels of wealth have been transferred out of the West into the Middle-East (and increasingly to China for cheap goods) and in return, that money has been used to finance the West's Government Bonds, and buy up their stock markets and real estate. As a result the Middle Eastern nations are second only to China in owning Western stocks, bond and real estate, and possibly have the ability to foreclose the Western economies should they wish to do so. We have then three diverse but interrelating influences

(1) the dependence on oil and the related need to maintain the artificial borders drawn

by Britain and France in the wake of the defeat of the Ottoman Empire at the end of WWI,

(2) the emerging economic and political power of the Islamic Nations, along with the pressure exerted by Islamic radicals,

(3) the decline in the cohesion and collective will of the Western Nations related to the deteriorating influence of historic Christianity especially among the decision making elite.

This confluence of influences has helped the West respond with an increasing lack of strategic clarity to a whole range of diverse issues.

Corruption in Africa and the Cold War

Political and economic corruption had become an institution before and during the colonial era. The, dignified exchange of gifts between rulers which had been an ancient African custom was exploited as a means of corruption. Then legitimate rulers who opposed European policy were deposed and new "Chieftaincies" were created to ensure better cooperation would be guaranteed. Even the justice system was perverted in cases in which colonial governments had an interest as happened with Jomo Kenyatta in Kenya.

During (and just after) the Cold War, several of the African nations formed from the former colonial empires were left to rot under often obscene dictatorships, frequently linked to the intelligence services of the West, who allowed these African "leaders" free reign, and helped prop them up as long as they gave at least the appearance of resisting the spread of communism on the African continent. There were also some African States with close ties to the Soviet Communist Block. Many of the African elite of this era were military officers, trained in the "East" or the "West" where several had reportedly been recruited by foreign intelligence services. The emerging political and middle classes were systematically decimated along with the economy. Intellectuals were hounded and health and education systems were allowed to decay through lack of funding. Political opponents were assassinated at home or even in exile.

Western corporations and their African cronies instituted the modern culture of impunity, disregard for the rule of law and the blatant corruption that would become the bane of the modern African nations. In the 1980s, jumbo loans were given to many developing nations as part of "Structural Adjustment Programmes" only to disappear without affecting the lives of ordinary people. Public owned economic assets were sold off usually to foreign owners and their local "partners". These combinations of loans and economic directives from abroad, also had the effect of undermining the sovereignty and the economic growth of these nations as well as stifling the grown of key areas like education and health as the jumbo loans were often "diverted" elsewhere.

This was also often a period of increasing instability in many of the African nations with military and other dictators becoming the only "glue" that held the nation together. A number of "proxy wars" were fought by these African satellites on behalf of their external puppet masters. Wars in Angola and Mozambique were examples of this. Many of these African dictators were also give cheap access to arms and ammunition to keep them safe in their often unpopular rule. Many of these are the arms and ammunition still floating around on the continent, continuing to cause death, injury and terror.

The preferential economic treatment of certain European corporations built during and after the Cold War would last for decades, and any of the "new breed" of African politicians who would later try to dismantle this structure, and allow young Africans a chance to aspire to the higher levels of international business, would often find themselves pitted against powerful and shady forces with the ability to affect the destiny of African nations.

Complex Conflicts

Some African leaders have also armed groups in neighbouring countries to protect their economic or political interests. France and America have armed both governments and other groups on the continent. The Soviet Union armed their own proxies and since the collapse of that Union, huge amounts of weaponry have been sold by former Soviet Republics; both to nations and to arm factions in various conflicts. The role China will play in the medium to longer term remains to be seen.

Not all conflicts in Africa are caused by extraction of resources. Africa is much more complex than simplistic explanations assert and many nations contain sub-groups, alliances and both traditional and emerging networks that remain mostly invisible to the foreign press and academia. The layer of extractive commodity conflict is often intertwined and overlaid onto other complex local conditions, including poverty and criminality. So for example, a long standing ethnic rivalry with historic grievances, may be manipulated in the efforts to exploit the extraction of local mineral or other resources. Poor local governance and weak central government may combine with ethnic, religious and political rivalries to provide conditions for conflict. In many cases, businesses outside Africa are the real winners!

Post-Cold-War conflicts had begun to decline in Africa with the ending of wars in Mozambique, Angola, Ethiopia and Chad; that is until the spike in violence by Boko Haram, AQIM, Al Shabbab and others. In some places (notably the Central African Republic) where the nominally Christian anti-Balaka have taken up arms against Moslem militias with some quite brutal effectiveness. While not endorsing this development, the action by anti-Balaka is perhaps a portent of increasing determination by young Christian men across Africa to arm themselves in resistance to what they see as forced Islamisation of their areas.

Sudan, the East of Congo and Somalia remain volatile. The destruction of Libya and the killing of Colonel Ghaddafi has left a vacuum in Central North Africa that has added arms and men trained to use them to the ranks of AQIM, Boko Haram and ISIS. At the time of writing Libya appeared to be slipping further into chaos with ISIS holding and even gaining territory there. However, the Liberia, Sierra Leone and other conflicts have ended, and many of the old Cold War proxy struggles are now only memories.

Africa is developing faster than ever before; but not as fast as the billions of young people on the continent would have wanted. Europe and the UN have evolved more effective negotiation and military interventions for the more "traditional" types of African civil war. There are fewer answers to the new kinds of wars appearing on the African Continent and elsewhere. Unfortunately these other continuing conflicts including the terrorist insurgencies like Boko Haram are seriously affecting the investment and development potential of large parts of Africa.

Poverty and underdevelopment are often given as underlying causes of conflicts, but the conflicts themselves are real deterrents to development. On the whole, African governments need to be more responsive to the needs of their people. The days of the unholy alliances between Western Banks, other multinational Corporations and corrupt African elites are numbered as new generations of social-media savvy, politically aware young people emerge across the continent. Western voters are also more ready to hold their elected officials to account for foreign policy and the behaviour of their national companies doing business abroad.

The next chapter begins to trace the rise and impact of ISIS and Boko Haram.

Chapter Seventeen – Boko Haram

Recent Origins

There are several claims as to the origin of Boko Haram. Most credible is that the original group who were more political and intellectual radicals, teamed up with other more violent groups of thugs. Some say that the new violent group had been armed and used by politicians in a previous election. They now became the muscle or enforcers for the earlier group of Islamic radicals who up to that point were mainly just philosophers and academics. Gradually and as a result of brutality and human rights abuses by successive Government agencies, the more violent members rose to lead the entire group.

Gangs without Hope

A similar story is told in several parts of Africa, where groups of unemployed young men and local criminals are mobilised for political or other purposes by some highly placed people, but the gangs later get out of control. In several of these versions, there are allegations that some of the gangs that later morph into insurgents or terrorists, went their own way after their original job was done, or their paymasters failed to pay them or both. Wikileaks brought in another rather far-fetched dimension, by accusing the US Government of secretly funding certain groups of radical Islamists as a means of destabilising Nigeria. That seems hard to believe, but in the realms of secret government operations, is not completely impossible.

Thousands, even millions of the people of North Eastern Nigeria have been victims of the terrorists called Boko Haram. Many are displaced, and many have lost their lives. But the problem of Boko

Haram did not start with Mohammed Yusuf. Varieties of Boko Haram have existed since 1903, more than 100 years.

Historic Origins

Boko Haram is only the latest manifestation of an old problem in Northern Nigeria, and no Government has succeeded in ending this problem. The Sokoto Caliphate, earlier founded for Islamic Jihad by Usman dan Fodio in 1804, was defeated by the British Army at Bauchi in 1903. The last independent Caliph, Attahiru I; died in that battle. His son Muhammad Bello and the surviving members of their army settled in Sudan, where their descendants still live. Every government in Nigeria since the British has also had this problem of cross border militant Islamist Jihad, in one form or another.

The Maitatsine Rebellion

In the 1980s there was a resurgence of the Maitatsine rebellion which had actually started under British rule before Nigeria's Independence. The Nigerian military only managed to suppress the Maitatsine "riots" in Kano and elsewhere after a massive loss of civilian life. The violence spiked further after Maitatsine himself was killed by Nigerian forces. Several of Maitatsine's followers known as Yan Tatsine, relocated to Maiduguri which was one of their strongholds and which would later become the base for Boko Haram.

Malam Musa Makaniki, the second in command of Maitatsine eventually escaped a manhunt in Nigeria by fleeing across the border to Cameroun from Maiduguri. This tactic of crossing the borders of neighbouring African states would later be employed very effectively by Boko Haram. Makaniki was captured later and jailed, but in 2012 he was freed "mysteriously" in Jos.

Kala Kato and the Nigerian "Taliban"

In the 1990s, we had the Kala Kato in Bauchi. In 2002 we had the Nigerian "Taliban". In 2011 we also had the Yusiffiya. Today we have Boko Haram, affiliated to ISIS. All these groups have operated within the same general location of Northern Nigeria and have found sanctuary across nearby borders especially Cameroun and Niger.

Mohammed Yusuf and Boko Haram

Mohammed Yusuf (1970 – 2009), founded the group known as Boko Haram in 2002 the official name of Boko Haram in Arabic is "Jama'atu Ahlis Sunna Lidda'awati wal-Jihad", which means "People Committed to the Propagation of the Prophet's Teachings and Jihad". Yusuf was a student of the Hanbalist brand of early Salafism established by Ahmad Ibn Taymiyyah and Ibn Qudamah in the 13th and 14th Centuries. Hanbalism, one of the most conservative and rigid schools of jurisprudence in Sunni Islam, is considered to be one of the strongest influences on modern Salafism, Wahhabism and Jihadism.

Yusuf was killed or perhaps summarily executed by the Nigerian Police in 2009, during unrest that left nearly 1000 people dead. The killing of Yusuf led to a further radicalisation of Boko Haram towards violence.

Between 2010 and 2013 Boko Haram's attacks then grew in sophistication as they began to receive inspiration and support from three other Salafist organisations, al-Qaeda in the Islamic Maghreb (AQIM), Somalia's al-Shabab (The Youth), and al-Qaeda in the Arabian Peninsula (AQAP). In March 2015, Boko Haram announced allegiance to ISIS, the self-declared Islamic State of Iraq and the Levant. ISIS also has branches in Libya and in West Africa. There had been persistent stories for several years of lighter skinned men, some possibly European and unable to speak the local Nigerian languages, who have been training Boko Haram fighters. Boko Haram also includes mercenaries and local criminals who do not have religious depth but are useful as "muscle" for the group.

The founder of Boko Haram Mohammed Yusuf, was an adopted son of one of the Maitatsine leaders. Maitatsine himself was a Cameroonian and used the Northern Region of that nation to stage his attacks within Nigeria. Boko Haram later made Northern Cameroun very much their home, crossing the border easily to attack Nigerian forces. With groups like Boko Haram and ISIS, it is important to think of them as ignoring the borders imposed by colonial empires, which is part of their raison d'être

The present Boko Haram is all of the former insurgencies and more, as an international group affiliated with ISIS, it has connections and support far beyond the borders of Nigeria. In North Africa and the Sahel today, you can get any kind of weapons you want because of the mess left by America and her allies in Libya. That is why (at least initially) some Boko Haram could be better armed than a small unit of regular soldiers. They have also captured weapons and ammunition stores on some their raids. There are also strong allegations that Boko Haram have been helped, even by people in the official security system. The USA and European nations reportedly refused to arm or help the Nigerian military on human rights grounds, while continuing to do big business comfortably with Saudi Arabia and other nations whose human rights have been questioned.

Boko Haram and Crude Oil

There have also been strong but persistent rumours that THE REAL REASON BOKO HARAM IS BEING USED AGAINST THE NIGERIAN GOVERNMENT, IS BECAUSE OF THE CRUDE OIL DISCOVERED AROUND LAKE CHAD!!! In this hypothetical scenario, some of those who are behind Boko Haram know that eventually the crude oil in Lake Chad area will become an international commodity. They will eventually try to force the Government to agree to their terms as part of a peace deal with Boko Haram.

The ideology of ISIS and its affiliates is characterised by "Apocalyptic Islam", which Joel Rosenberg defines as even more dangerous than the Radical Islam which has existed in some form since the religion emerged in the 16th Century. Rosenberg is of the opinion that a controversial, apocalyptic Islamic eschatology crosses over between Iran which is Shia, and ISIS which is Sunni; both believing that we are living in the end times when the Islamic Messiah or Mahdi will appear to rule the Earth with Jesus Christ as his deputy! According to Rosenberg, this apocalyptic Islamic view believes that attacking Jews, Christians, America and Israel etc. will make these events happen much faster!

According to Carl LeVan, victory over Boko Haram is more than conquering territory, and must include winning over their ideology, and also redefining the future role of Islam in the multi-ethnic, multi-faith context found in sub-Saharan Africa.

Outside of the Middle East and Western Asia, Africa is the area where Islam has the greatest areas of land and the largest populations. Particularly if ISIS is eventually denied their haven in Iraq and Syria, we can expect that their affiliates in Africa, including Boko Haram and those in Egypt, Libya, Tunisia and elsewhere will then become even more of a problem than they are today.

The next chapter looks at the influence of the movements to abolish slavery and the impact of their work on the efforts to evangelise sub-Saharan Africa.

Chapter Eighteen – African's Return as Christian Missionaries

19th Century European Missions

Roman Catholic missions to Africa in the 19th Century were mainly renewed activities of the Holy Ghost Fathers, as well as the Society of the African Missions and the Missionary Society of the White Fathers. The German Society of the Divine Word was also in the mission field. In spite of the considerable efforts of European missionaries to convert Africans, the real and lasting missionary successes would come when native Africans, including former slaves returned to Africa.

For many of the European missionaries it would often appear that the Christianity they preached was only accepted superficially by Africans, and sometimes as a means of accessing modern health care or education or some other benefit provided by the church. Many Christian converts were suspected of continuing in their old African traditional religious practises in secret, including the veneration of ancestors; especially in times of crisis. Even Bishop Ajayi Crowther, himself born in Africa and rescued from a slave ship complained about the influence of the priests of the native religion over the people. These problems still have their modern equivalent in many parts of Africa, Asia and South America. In spite of the difficulties and the dangers of disease, war and lack of communications, many European missionaries gave years of dedicated service to Africa and laid the foundation for the spread of Christianity on that continent today. Many would give their lives for the Gospel and lie buried in cemeteries across Africa.

Abolitionist Missionaries

Another phase of missionary activity to Africa was rooted in the abolitionist battles to end the trade in enslaved Africans. James Oglethorpe was an early pioneer of abolition and was followed by his friends Granville Sharp, Hannah More, Henry Venn and William Wilberforce and many others who founded the revivalist Clapham Sect at All Saints Church in London. This small group of Christians became a huge influence on Britain and the entire world, through the strength of their moral and spiritual values. Their influence included politics as they took up the cause of abolition of slavery led by William Wilberforce and several prominent Black campaigners like Olaudah Equiano, also supported their efforts as did the Bishop of London.

The Clapham Saints also campaigned for reform of the prisons and founded missionary and Christian publications. They were instrumental to the creation of the Sierra Leone colony for freed slaves with a plan that this would become the base for training former enslaved Africans as missionaries.

In 1807, largely through the Clapham Saints and their allies, including freed Africans like Ouladah Equiano, Parliament in London passed the Slave

Trade Act which prohibited slave trading in all of the British Empire. And in 1883 Parliament finally passed the Slavery Abolition Act, which emancipated slaves in all parts of the Empire. The influence of the small group of Christians changed the moral outlook of their nation and helped create the morality of Victorian Britain. There was a parallel movement in the USA and in other countries (notably The Society of the Friends of the Blacks or Société des amis des Noirs) in France, but the Clapham Saints also succeeded in persuading the British Government to use their navy and other resources to help end slavery. Some modern human rights organisations like Anti-Slavery International can be traced back to the work of the British abolitionists.

The London Missionary Society founded by the Clapham Saints would play a major role in the next wave of African evangelism. German, French and Swiss Protestants also sent missionaries out to Africa. Sierra Leone was founded as a haven for freed slaves (1787), and Fourah Bay College established there would help produce many missionaries for the evangelisation of Africa, most famous among them was Samuel Ajayi Crowther, a former slave. Crowther was the very first student (1827) at Fourah bay. He was ordained an Anglican Priest in 1843 in London and consecrated a Bishop in 1864. He was the head of the Niger Mission of the Church Missionary Society from 1857.

Slave Rebellions

Between 1526 and 1859 there are at least 23 significant rebellions by enslaved Africans recorded in North America and the Caribbean, many of them successful to some degree. Among the most famous of these are:

- Haitian Revolution (French Saint-Domingue), 1791–1804

- Nat Turner's rebellion (Virginia) 1831

- Baptist War (British Jamaica) 1831–1832

- John Brown's Raid (Virginia) 1859

The abolition movement also coincided with or even inspired some of the rebellions by the enslaved Africans, who rose up to demand their freedom. One of the most well-known of these happened at Christmas 1831 and is remembered as the "Baptist War". Samuel Sharpe, the Baptist Preacher, had organised the protest as a peaceful strike action but the situation degenerated when their demand to be paid half the wages of free white workers were rejected. The local militia and the British Army were deployed against the angry Black slaves and violence raged for about ten days. This extended loss of life and destruction caused two parliamentary inquiries in London and helped set the stage for the eventual passing of the 1833 Slavery Abolition Act.

Returning African Missionaries

We shall see more examples of how Africans returning from the Americas and the Caribbean, and local African evangelists and missionaries would make the key difference in carrying the gospel beyond the coast, the main cities and the elite into the interior of Africa and into the lives of ordinary Africans. This is not to depreciate in any way the efforts of European and other missionaries, but to balance the picture which has persisted in history that it was Europeans who bore the bulk of the evangelisation of Africa.

Several Africans who had been taken as slaves or were descended from slaves returned to help evangelise Africa. Along with indigenous African missionaries, they were to transform the evangelisation of Africa. Some of those African American Missionaries who returned to Africa or helped establish missions in Africa; included:

Albert P. Miller served the West African Mendi Mission for 3 years. He graduated from Yale and later pastored a Congregational Church in New Haven. David George ministered to the Black communities in Nova Scotia, before travelling to

Sierra Leone to become a Christian leader there. David George had earlier served in the Silver Bluff, S.C. Baptist Church, known as the earliest Black Baptist Church in the USA. James W. C. Pennington, the "First Black Student" at Yale University (1830s) helped to form the Mendi Mission, founded in Sierra Leone for the 35 survivors of the Amistad revolt.

Several African-Americans were sent to Africa as missionaries by the African Baptist Missionary Society formed in 1815 by Lott Carey (a former slave) and others. Carey led a missionary team to Sierra Leone and from there to Monrovia Liberia where he founded the Providence Baptist Church, the first church planted there to minister to the African-American settlers and the local Africans. In 1897, a group of African-American Baptists founded the Lott Carey Foreign Mission Convention, (named after Lott Carey) which is still active in Christian mission in Africa, over 100 years later.

Edward Blyden a Presbyterian minister became a high school principal in Liberia and edited a local paper. Alexander Crummell studied at Yale University (unofficially) and at Queens College Cambridge. He served as an Episcopal Church missionary in Liberia for twenty years. He had earlier served as the Pastor of St. Luke's Episcopal Church, New Haven a congregation that continues till this day.

Orishatukeh Faduma also graduated from Yale and went on to do graduate studies there. Born in Liberia to African parents, Faduma, worked as a missionary and educator in the South of the USA and in West Africa for nearly 50 years.

Amanda Smith (1837-1915), a former slave, spent nearly a dozen years abroad as an evangelist and missionary for the African Methodist Episcopal Church, working in England, India and Monrovia before returning to the USA to found an orphanage. The AME Church, founded by former slave Richard Allen, has remained one of the most active in African Christian missions. Maria Fearing another former slave went to the Congo as a missionary when she was 56 years old! She had learned to read and write at 33 and then went to school to become a qualified teacher!

William Henry Sheppard (1865-1927) spent 20 years as a missionary in the Congo and around Central Africa. A pioneer African-American missionary for the Presbyterian Church, Sheppard told the world about the harsh treatment the Belgian colonizers gave to the local people in the Congo including cutting off their hands if they refused to work. For exposing the oppression of the local people to the world, Sheppard became known as "the Black Livingstone".

Josephus R. Coan, a missionary to South Africa for 12 years, also graduated from Yale and later taught in Atlanta at the Interdenominational Theological Center. Coan died in 2004, aged 101. Another returning African American woman Leila January founded the Lighthouse Full Gospel

Church in Monrovia in 1936. This Pentecostal church was later handed over to a local born Pastor Mother Frances Blatch.

The next chapter looks at the sometimes very difficult relationship between Islam and Christianity on the African continent, using Egypt and Northern Nigeria as our "case study".

Chapter Nineteen – Islam and Christianity in Egypt and Northern Nigeria

Islam came to the Hausaland Kingdom of City States in the 14th Century through what is thought to be the first Jihad. This was led by Sultan Ali Yaji of Kano, and resulted in a number of Hausa "Sultanates". However, Islam remained a religion mainly of the elite and many of the ordinary people retained their affiliation to the local (Boro) religions. The Fulani led Jihad of Usman dan Fodio would bring some reforms, but Islam in Northern Nigeria has historically gone through cycles of reform and returns to syncretism, involving African traditional religions. There have also always been some Moslem scholars who would view Western education and culture, and elements of Sufism in Islam (for example) with suspicion as forms of liberalisation of their religion.

A well-known advocate of the Islamisation of Nigeria was the hardliner Sheikh Abubakar Gumi, the Grand Khadi of Northern Nigeria from 1962 until that position was abolished in 1967. Sheikh Abubakar Gumi and Sheikh Ismaila Idris, are examples of leaders among Nigerian Islamic scholars who sought to bring back a purer form of Islam and reduce the influence of Western education through establishing the movement known as Izala. This movement like several others, was related to and often funded from the Saudi Arabian Salafist (Wahhabi) and Sahwa (Awakening) organisations in the Gulf. It is logical and possible to see a continuity of thought, from the ideals of purifying Islam promoted by organisations like Sahwa and Izala, and the later rise of other more fundamentalist and sometimes violent groups, like Ansaru and Boko Haram in Northern Nigeria.

With his reputation earlier built on opposition to British colonial rule, the Sheikh continued to criticise all forms of government other than Sharia and all forms of "westernisation" well into the 1980s. He was also against Sufism and other syncretistic groups within Islam. Sheikh Gumi, although quite different in methodology from Boko Haram, the teaching and preaching of Sheikh Gumi (and others like him), proves that the rejectionist strand against western education and influence in Northern Nigeria is certainly not a new innovation. Like Boko haram, Sheikh Gumi was able to use the benefits of the Western education system and the availability of mass media in ways that his predecessors and contemporaries could not. You can draw a direct line from the Sheikh's mastery of the media to that displayed by modern radical Islamists like ISIS and their affiliate, Boko Haram. . Academics and other intellectuals who may not advocate particular violent actions, may however set the foundations for others who come later and take their ideas much further.

At the time of writing, Sheikh Gumi is now elderly and seems to have mellowed some of his more fiery rhetoric, but he remains a strong critic of

Nigerian politicians and the violent methods of Boko Haram.

Christianity Under Islam

Contrary to some historical accounts, Christianity was not totally wiped out in Moslem North Africa, but its presence and power were greatly diminished under Islamic rule. Some Moslem rulers were more benign than others, but the southward move of Christianity in Africa from the Mediterranean was effectively ended. Although the number of Bishoprics declined dramatically, pockets of Christianity remained in the west of North Africa for hundreds of years, after the area was dominated by Islam. In the West of North Africa, some communities stayed connected to Rome and very few remain. In the East, principally in Egypt and Ethiopia, the Monastic tradition provided the church there with an additional strength and depth.

In his 2014 book "Nationalism and the Politics of National Security: The Christian And The Boko Haram Challenge", Pastor Ayo Oritsejafor, President, Christian Association of Nigeria (CAN) agrees that the current problems of Boko Haram can be traced back to some deep and historic divisions that have long been the cause of contention. He shows how the expansion of the Usman dan Fodio Jihad Southward from Sokoto was stopped by the Yoruba armies (Oyo) at Ilorin, a city that would later be won over to the Jihadists by "subterfuge" and the move Eastward towards old Kanem-Bornu by Muhammed ibn el-Kanemi. Of mixed Kanembu and Arab heritage, Muhammed ibn el-Kanemi rallied the Kenembu of Chad (who are closely related to the Kanuri) and the Baggāra (Shuwa/Diffa) Arabs from today's Sudan. Together this alliance defeated the armies of the Sokoto Jihad, before El Kanemi was ousted by the Mahdists forces of Sudan. Mahdist control of the North East of today's Nigeria was brief before defeat by a combination of French and British force. The British were not shy to install rulers of their own choice in both Sokoto and Maiduguri.

Persecution of Christians in Africa

The extent of Christian freedom in Islamic Africa often depended on the local Islamic rulers. During the reign of the Almohads and the Almoravids for example, Christians suffered a higher degree of persecution and many were forced to convert. By the time of French colonisation of North Africa in the mid-1800s there was almost no organised Christianity left in the areas they controlled. Most people who then became Christians in the French held areas, were connected with the colonial expatriate community and the majority left once independence came.

Much has been written about the areas of similarity and even agreement between Islam and Christianity for example that most of the people named in the Koran (including the Virgin Mary) are already named in the Bible. The Koran also agrees that Jesus will return to judge the world and many Sufi Moslems see Jesus as their mystical inspiration. Examples are given of Gulf States today who allow Christian worship for the Christian servants and migrant workers without whom their nations would not run. Christianity is allowed in that context as long as there is no proselytizing among the native Moslem population. It is claimed that Christians and Jews have been able to live peacefully under Moslem rule at different times through history (especially in the Middle Ages), but it is also true that there have been times when that relationship has been very bad indeed.

Dhimmi Taxes for non-Moslems

Historically, Non-Moslems living under Sharia Law had to pay special taxes (Dhimmi) and did not have the same rights as Moslems in that state. They could hold religious services, subject to restrictions, and could even have their own courts. Dhimmi are not expected to observe Moslem dietary laws. Islamic scholars disagree as to whether this practice of Dhimmi can be applied in a modern setting. In spite of these attempts at often uneasy coexistence, there have been cycles of violence caused by extremism, mainly either within Christianity or Islam. There have been atrocities by Christian groups against Moslems as in the 1995 Serbian massacre of Bosnian Moslems at Srebrnica. The war in Sudan has been one of the bloodiest Africa has ever seen. Interreligious wars also have implications on the status of women and for gender relations more widely.

Christian Persecution in Egypt

Founded by St Mark the Apostle, the Egyptian Orthodox Christians known as Copts have suffered persecution since Roman times. This maltreatment reached its height in the 3rd Century reign of Emperor Diocletian. That season of Coptic history is known as the "Era of the martyrs". Several of the early African monks like St Antony the Great, who pioneered the practices of monasticism, were driven into the Egyptian Desert to escape these persecutions. Even after Moslem (Arab) conquest in around 640AD, Egypt remained a Christian majority country and in spite of further persecutions by the new Arab rulers, Egypt did not become a Moslem majority country till late in the 14th Century.

Around 20% of the Egyptian population are Christian. The more recent persecution of Coptic Christians has been documented by Human Rights Watch. Christian children may also be made to learn and practice Islam while at school. The kidnapping of Coptic women who may never be seen again, or who may then reappear claiming to have converted to Islam and possibly "married" to a Moslem. Others remain in domestic servitude where they are the victims of physical, psychological and sexual abuse. The Moslem dominated Egyptian Government has long been accused of failing to investigate these cases or punish the culprits.

In 2010 a bipartisan group of 17 American Lawmakers demanded the American State

Department should confront Egypt on the scale and nature of these crimes against Christian women in Egypt. As with its often selective approach to human rights around the world, the USA continues to claim that it raises these kinds of "sensitive" issues "in private".

Other problems between the Moslem dominated Government of Egypt and the Coptic Orthodox Church include:

- Interference in the church including attempts to remove senior clergy

- Withholding compulsory permits for buying of land and building or repairing churches

- Missionaries restricted to community projects and banned from open preaching

- Non-recognition of conversions from Islam to Christianity

- Non-recognition of marriages between Christians and Moslems

- Children of such interfaith marriages must be registered as Moslems

Bombings, Murders, Massacres, Kidnappings

Bombings, murders, massacres, kidnappings and many other attacks against Christians, simply because of their faith have been repeatedly recorded in Egypt. Few if any of the culprits are ever found, arrested, prosecuted or convicted. Tourists have also become targets in recent years, with attacks from militant Islamists, including the bombing of an entire plane full Russian tourists over the Sinai in 2015. The period known as the Arab Spring beginning from 2010 became a particularly difficult time for the Copts of Egypt. Recent years have seen a rise in militancy among Egypt's Moslems. The Egyptian Army has also been accused of committing atrocities against Coptic Christians, including the murder of 24 unarmed Copts in 2011, in the "Maspero massacre".

Persecution of Christians in Nigeria

In between the areas controlled by these armies of Sokoto, Oyo and Kanem-Bornu, Christian missionaries were able to continue working, winning converts from the largely animist peoples and building churches. As a result of this missionary activity, many of these communities in what is known as the Middle Belt of Nigeria (between the far north and the South) have remained Christian up till the present day. Over the years they have come under increasing pressure from Islam.

Although the British Army finally defeated the Caliphate established by Usman dan Fodio when they entered Sokoto in 1903, the British continued to rule the area through the Emirate system established by Usman. European Colonial Empires were notoriously short of manpower, with only a handful of European ruling over far flung territories often containing hundreds of thousands and even millions of natives.

One strategy used to even out the lack of colonial manpower was the famous system of "divide and rule", which set different local groups against each other so that they could not unite against the colonial ruler, who then played peacemaker. Another tactic was the "indirect rule" which used native rulers to rule on behalf of the coloniser. In many areas of Empire, Islamic rulers seemed to be a ready-made solution for the colonisers, often with government structures (Emirates), a system of law (Sharia), and their own local armies to do the colonisers bidding, at a price. That price often included allowing the local Moslem leader jurisdiction over people who were not Moslem, and often included Christians.

Building of roads and railways by colonial powers assisted the spread of Islam in remote areas of West Africa. Some of the labourers brought into Africa by the British colonial rulers were also Moslems from Asia and this helped spread Islam in some parts of Southern Africa. Moslem soldiers, helped enforce the "Pax Coloniala" especially in

West Africa. The remoteness of nominally Christian centres of the Empires and the need for order in the territories, often meant that the European Empires were themselves responsible for helping spread Islam in Africa and placing even more Africans under Islamic rule.

In Moslem dominated areas of Northern Nigeria there have been long term and persistent rumours that children going through the school system, are discriminated against on the basis of religion. For example CAN claims that Christian religious education is routinely banned in Northern schools. A 2015 investigation by the Christian Association of Nigeria showed that Northern Moslem students are routinely promoted or given preference of admission to schools and academic courses over their Christian counterparts, even when the latter are better qualified. The CAN investigation showed that this practice was found in the following Northern Nigerian states.

- Adamawa

- Bauchi
- Bornu
- Gombe
- Kaduna
- Kano
- Kebbi
- Niger
- Taraba
- Yobe
- Zamfara

The CAN report also found that Christians in Northern Nigeria are discriminated against in employment as well, citing the case of several government agencies that are routinely and continuously headed by Northern Moslems such as the Nigerian Ports Authority (NPA). The CAN report claims that this practice extends to the Police and other agencies and was entrenched during the years of Islamic military dictatorship.

According to CAN, many Christians in Northern Nigeria are forced to change their names to sound more Moslem and sometimes they have no choice but to convert to Islam.

Political Discrimination

CAN also reports on the political discrimination against Christians. After the Kafanchan Crisis of 1987 governments in Northern Nigeria began to create separate areas for Christians and Moslems to live where none had existed before. This crisis also market the accelerated conversion of Christian Chiefdoms in Northern Nigeria into "Emirates" by government order. The CAN report lists a number of these historically Christian areas, which had never been conquered during the earlier Islamic Jihads, but that were now forcibly Islamised, by being suddenly declared "Emirates", which included:

- Minna

- Dass

- Gwoza

- Askirah

- Zur

- Uba

- Birnin – Gwari

- Lere (in Kaduna state)

- Ganye

After the Christian areas of Northern Nigeria were declared "Emirates" there was reportedly a further relocation of Moslems from other areas, some from as far as the neighbouring country of Chad in order to permanently change the demographics of the new "Emirates" and provide a ready power base for the newly appointed Moslem ruler. The building of churches and the teaching of Christian religion was often made difficult and sometimes Christianity was virtually driven underground. Generally, Moslems practice their religion everywhere in Nigeria without fear of harassment. The same cannot be said for Christians and this has been true for many years. There are many parts of Northern Nigeria where you cannot carry the Holy Bible in the street, you hide it in a bag on your way to and from church!

Several of these new "Emirates" in Nigeria have then continued to be the areas with high levels of intimidation and even violence against Christians, and these areas have also been specially targeted by Boko Haram, as in the now infamous case of the kidnapping of the nearly 300 Christian Chibok Girls.

300 Christian Chibok Girls Kidnapped!

As reported by Adam Nossiter of the New York Times and other journalists the majority of the Chibok Girls kidnapped by Boko Haram, are Christians. Their home in Chibok is one of the Christian areas of Northern Nigeria which had only small minority of Moslems! As such it was a particular target for Boko Haram, especially the girls' school. There are as yet unsubstantiated rumours that certain highly placed people in the local community including officials in the education system mysteriously took their daughters out of the Chibok boarding school, the night that Boko Haram came... Security had also reportedly been reduced in the area...These all remain to be investigated, if they ever will. Even with the dismal record on security that most African Governments have, these are the kinds of additional dangers that Christians in Moslem areas of Africa can be faced with.

Another report by the Christian Association of Nigeria (CAN) confirmed that these girls kidnapped by the ISIS affiliate Boko Haram were mostly Christian. The CAN report published the names of the missing girls, which included names like Deborah, Mary, Gloria, Tabitha, Ruth, Esther and Anthonia, and with surnames like Ezekiel and James showing clearly their Christian rather than Moslem religious affiliation. As many Christians in

Moslem parts of Africa routinely take on Islamic names to smooth their way through life, it is also possible that even the girls with Moslem sounding names were also Christians. STRANGELY, THE WESTERN MEDIA FOUND IT IMPOSSIBLE TO MENTION THAT THE CHIBOK GIRLS WERE CHRISTIANS DELIBERATELY KIDNAPPED BY ISLAMIC TERRORISTS!

Other Abductions of Christians

According to another CAN report, there had in fact been a steady stream of abductions of Christian youth (male and female) in Northern Nigeria going back many years. Those abducted were often taken into mosques, never to be seen again or to re-emerge claiming to have converted to Islam, and in the case of young Christian girls, mysteriously "married" to Moslem men. The Sultan Bello Mosque in Kaduna has reportedly been known for years as one of the most notorious for "converting" young Christians by financial inducements or even by force. Security services in

Northern Nigeria have allegedly appeared powerless to act on complaints by Christian parents and family. The Moslem dominated military dictatorships which ruled Nigeria in the past turned a "blind eye" or even sided quietly with the abductors.

The North of Nigeria was initially reluctant to join in the Nigeria being created at the end of colonial rule. In 1953 Moslems in what is now the North of Nigeria were strongly opposed to the granting of independence to a multi ethnic and multi-faith Nigeria by Britain. They wanted their own Islamic state. Feeling provoked by the campaigning of the mainly Christian Southern politicians, Moslem Northerners rioted and targeted Christians living in the North. Both Northerners and Southerners died or were injured in those 1953 clashes.

There have also been tensions between the mainly Sunni Moslems in Nigeria and the minority Shia (Shiites). There have also been problems between the Shia and the Nigerian Government from time-to-time. In january 2016, the leader of the Shiite Islamic Movement of Nigeria (IMN) Sheikh Ibrahim al-Zakzaky, remains in detention in Nigeria, recovering from what he claims were serious injuries from six bullets that allegedly hit him during a raid by the Nigerian Government on his home. The raid followed the most recent clash between the IMN and the Nigerian Government in which a large number of Shia are alleged to have been killed. The BBC and other news media have reported extensively on these clashes.

Sharia Law Introduced

By 2012, Sharia Law had been unilaterally introduced in 12 Nigerian States since the trend began in 1999, when the then Governor of Zamfara State, Ahmad Rufai Sani started the trend towards Sharia implementation in Nigeria. So far, 9 of Sharia States in Nigeria have a majority of Moslems (often with a substantial Christian population), and a further 3 have a broader mix of Moslems, Christians and others. Most Nigerian Moslems are Sunni. The 12 original Sharia states in Northern Nigeria were:

1. Bauchi

2. Bornu

3. Gombe

4. Jigawa

5. Kaduna

6. Kano

7. Katsina

8. Kebbi

9. Niger

10. Sokoto

11. Yobe

12. Zamfara

In all of these States there have also been populations of Christians as well as Moslems. Some commentators claim that implementing Sharia is in violation of Nigeria's Constitution. Three of these Kaduna, Niger and Gombe were not wholly Moslem states at the time Sharia was instituted. In fact Kaduna State has always had a substantial Christian population in the southern part of the state.

In the aftermath of President Johnathan losing to President Buhari in the 2015 elections in Nigeria, Churches were burnt and at least 100 Christians were reported killed in Sokoto, Kaduna and other States. There were no reports of burning of mosques in the South. Although that violence was fairly quickly contained, it shows again the level of intimidation under which Christians in Moslem Northern Nigeria and elsewhere in Africa and the Middle East (for example) have to live on a daily basis. Sharia had been the cause of conflict elsewhere. The introduction of Sharia Law in the Sudan in 1983 by President Gaafar Nimieri, was a major trigger for renewed outbreak of war in that nation.

Statements by the Christian Association of Nigeria (CAN) endorsed by the President of CAN Pastor Ayo Oritsejafor, claimed that the displacement of greater numbers of Christians by Boko Haram in the run-up to the 2015 Nigerian Presidential Elections, was a factor in the "landslide" victories in the Northern States of Nigeria, by President Muhammadu Buhari.

The great challenge for Africa (and some other regions of the world) has been in finding ways to replace the violent responses of insurgency, terrorism and civil war, with the gentler processes of institutionalised democracy. Africa is in need of statesmen and women who refuse to spill the blood of their fellow citizens in pursuit of their political ambitions. The willing acceptance of defeat by Dr Goodluck Jonathan in the 2015 presidential election in Nigeria, set a remarkable example of gallantry, in spite of allegations of vote rigging on both sides, but especially in the far North of that country.

Death and Displacement

Some estimates on Wikipedia show that deaths from religious violence in Northern Nigeria between 2000 and 2015, may have totalled more than 20,000 people killed, involving both Moslem and Christians! Since the Christians are a minority in the North of Nigeria and are often targeted deliberately in such violence, it is clear that Christians will be disproportionately represented in the resulting deaths and injuries. They will also have lost a greater amount of property in proportion to their numbers and will also be in disproportionately higher numbers among the 2.3 million people displaced from their homes by the insurgency. The Western Press largely avoids reporting on this and Western political and religious leaders are mostly silent...

To these figures we would need to add the other deaths in religious violence from the 1950s the massacres of Christian Southerners in the 1960s and all the many other seasons of religious violence from Maitatsine through to the Kalo Kato Uprising. The totals numbers of people killed in religious violence in Northern Nigeria is truly staggering and certainly the impact on Christians in the region remains under-reported.

The Nigerian Civil War (Biafra)

The story of Christian Nigeria would not be complete without remembering the nearly six-months-long massacres of mainly Christian South-Easterners living in the North in 1966. The atrocities committed at that time including the mass rape of Southern Christian women by rampaging Northern gangs have been well documented. There were no corresponding levels of violence against Northern Moslems living in the South.

There were also accusations that some Christians in the "Middle Belt" joined northern Moslems in attacking Eastern Christians during these terrible times. However some few Moslems also helped save some Christians. Many more Eastern Nigerian Christians would die in the civil war that followed a declaration of secession by mainly Christian South East of the country who had now declared the new nation of "Biafra". Estimates vary from about 1.5 million to over 3 million DEAD! The civil war (failed Biafran war of independence) pitted a predominantly Moslem army (backed by Britain) against a mainly Ibo Christian South East.

The war itself was to be marred by allegations of war crimes for which no one has ever stood trial including rape as a weapon of war, mass starvation and bombing of civilians, and massacres such as those at Asaba which have been well researched, and in which up to 1000 mainly Christian men and boys were machine gunned to death and the entire city ravaged. The massacre at Asaba was preceded by other such crimes (in Warri, and Benin etc.) as the Federal Army pushed the "Biafrans" back from advancing on the federal capital of Lagos. Unfortunately, the "Biafran" Army also retaliated by killing non-Ibo civilians as they retreated. That is the madness of war, but none of those crimes (and many others) have ever been accounted for. Many people in those traumatic times turned to the churches for comfort.

Revival from the Ashes

The failed war of "Biafran Independence" led to a rise in "prophetic churches" as people sought spiritual safety as a sanctuary from physical danger. African prophetic churches are now found all over the world, but have remained confined to the expatriate African communities who host them. There was also a rise in Pentecostal churches immediately after the war. It is possible that a kind of spiritual revival, born in the anguish of that war, later spread across many other parts of Nigeria as many of the early Pentecostal preachers of the post-war period came from the war affected areas.

The conflicts, corruption, economic hardship and general insecurity of the decades following independence drove many people to seeking spiritual answers to problems in their own lives and in their nations. Pentecostal churches have helped provide people with those spiritual "choices". There is another view that Pentecostal churches have become a means of self-enrichment by those who lead them! There are some possible proofs of that view, but the robust Pentecostalism born in the trials and tribulations of life in Nigeria has become one of the strongest modern church groups in the world.

"The Politics of National Security"

In his 2014 book "Nationalism and the Politics of National Security: The Christian And The Boko Haram Challenge", Pastor Ayo Oritsejafor, President, Christian Association of Nigeria (CAN) repeatedly accuses generations of Moslem leaders in Northern Nigeria of putting the advance of their religion above the best interests of the nation. He believes and presents his case that Moslem leaders in Nigeria have an agenda to perpetuate their rule and to complete a jihad across the entire country. Many others would argue against his views, but there are plenty to agree with him. Pastor Ayo also more broadly blames the Nigerian and African political elite for the failures of Africa. His critics say he is part of that failed elite himself.

Pastor Ayo (as he is popularly known) also agrees with commentators who see Nigeria (and other parts of Africa) as the true current battleground of a global struggle between Western Civilisation and Islam. In this model or mode of thinking held by Pastor Ayo and others, both "moderate" and "radical" Islam are a problem to African Christianity, in that both oppose the spread of the Gospel on the continent. Those who subscribe to this view would say that the problem for Christianity is only a matter of degree and that the milder form of Islam often only paves the way for a more hard line version.

Islamist attacks in Europe and America may make the headlines, but only outside the West and particularly in Africa, and parts of the Middle East, does radical Islam have both the numbers on the ground and the vast stretches of territory to enable the establishment the radical Islamic states they desire to hold and operate from. Far from being a quick and easy task, the fight against ISIS, Al Shabab, Boko Haram, Al Qaeda in the Maghreb and others in Africa, may last for many years to come

Christianity generally accepts a degree of separation of church and state and therefore a secular society. Islam however is usually comprehensively intertwined into all aspects of life. The two religions therefore have the potential for disagreement on the very nature of society. This does not mean that the two religions cannot co-exist, but that misunderstandings are likely, and can be exploited by those for whom conflict is profitable. On the whole, Christians have historically tended to take the passive and liberal view towards Islam, with mainly counter-attacks in response to earlier invasions or other incidents. Most of the world seems to have forgotten that Moslem armies invaded Europe long before the so called "Crusades" were organised to chase them out and back into the Middle East! Today the

"Crusades" are spoken of purely as an attack on Islam by the Christian West!

What then is the future of Africa with Christianity and the Bible? Next, in our final chapter, we reflect on aspects of the previous chapters and look at the unfolding global destiny of Africa.

Chapter Twenty – Africa's Future Destiny

Pentecostalism is largely an African phenomenon, whose substance and energy has come from the descendants of Africa all over the world. This Pentecostal movement has also affected the historic church denominations in Africa (and elsewhere) most profoundly, forcing them to innovate or lose their members to the Pentecostals. The robust theological stance that has differentiated African Anglicans from much of the wider Communion for example; is partly as a result of the presence among them of vibrant Pentecostal churches. But when will they start truly working together?

Pentecostalism

Pentecostals generally take a high view of scripture and expect a second blessing or baptism in the Holy Spirit after conversion. The Holy Spirit then imparts gifts to the believer for Christian service, typically including a "gift of tongues". For the church leaders who affiliate with the Apostolic Pastoral Congress, holiness of life and conduct is the main evidence of baptism in the Holy Spirit. Pentecostals generally also accept divine healing, dreams, and visions. Pentecostal church services are often lively, and characterized by spontaneity and involvement of the congregation. However in recent years many Pentecostals have also been re-discovering sacraments, liturgy and vestments. They tend to have a high view of heterosexual marriage for life as an ideal, and most would feel that it is the Western churches and society who are almost obsessed with sex. Turn on a Hollywood movie or European TV show, and see how long before your mind is being led in that direction…

There is a huge diversity among the African churches. For example, Western academics have laboured to prove that the African Instituted Churches are also Pentecostal and need to be placed in the same category as the other Pentecostals. These studies have concentrated on what the Western scholars see as the similarities rather than the deep rooted differences and are actually quite misleading. These studies also run the risk of being seen as another case of the Western academic theologians telling the rest of the Christian world who they are, what they ought to think of themselves, and how they ought to behave and run their churches. Having said all that, we cannot tell the story of Pentecostalism without acknowledging the contribution to this modern revival by the Hamitic people, the sons and daughters of Africa.

Afro-Pentecostalism

Amos Yong and Estrelda Alexander edited the 2011 book titled Afro-Pentecostalism – Black Pentecostal and Charismatic Christianity in History and Culture, which traces the contributions of the African descendants of Ham, to the global Pentecostal movement from its birth in 1906 up to the centenary in 2006. The fourteen scholars whose essays are in the book, show how Black Christians (beginning with African Americans) have provided globally significant leadership in the development of Pentecostal theology and practice of musical and other worship, as well as their expository preaching style, and community engagement

There are certainly still gaps and tensions in Pentecostal academic scholarship. We celebrate the success of Azusa Street in connecting with and embracing the complexities of the multiple ethnicities and other identities in the America of the early 20th Century. At the same time, Azusa Street is almost always considered by academics as a multi-ethnic congregation first, rather than in its primarily African American origins.

Yong and Alexander's book also makes clear how innovative early Pentecostalism was, even among the African American communities who were then predominantly Baptist or Methodist.

Pentecostalism did not just change the way we worship. It also challenged a number of theological and practical perspectives, through a dynamically evolving context of Scripture and inspiration, to re-imagine church and community leadership; such as the role of women in church leadership, and issues of race, background, education or social class of those who lead Pentecostal congregations.

- Gender (particularly for women)
- Race (for Black and Asian people)
- Class (in a racially and financially divided America)

Pentecostalism therefore does not just liberate spiritually, but also transforms psychologically and socially. Pentecostalism has grown from its roots to influence not just the Christian religion, but also popular culture and general ideas on spirituality in the modern world. In the changing cultural environment and individual isolation of our modern times, Pentecostalism empowers often disenfranchised men and women by providing new biblical identities and Christian rites of passage, which offer the transition into these identities and affirm the recipient within a given community.

In other words, Pentecostalism provides a series of valid social, psycho-spiritual concepts not just for the members of a church, but holds possible paradigms for understanding and successfully navigating the multi-ethnic urban context of modern life. Pentecostals themselves need to understand these gifts better and perhaps discern a more universal (and sometimes specific) language to express these gifts in order to find their prophetic voice in the public square.

There is also a tension between the aspirational nature of much of modern Pentecostalism, found significantly in the "Prosperity Gospel" and the biblical role of the social-ethical prophet who speaks on behalf of the poor and the marginalised. In several African nations, such as in Kenya, churches (principally Anglican) have been quite bold in speaking truth to power.

Yong and Alexander's book also recognises the emergence of a new understanding, that Pentecostal praxis flows from a definitive theology which needs to be better articulated and which must perhaps have a clearer pneumatology, in order to express the centrality of the Holy Spirit in Pentecostalism. African Pentecostals have made (and are still making) very valid contributions to this Pentecostal movement, not just on the continent of Africa, but around the world. In many parts of Africa, the rise of Pentecostalism has challenged and given new energy to the historic denominations like the Roman Catholics and the Anglicans, who have had to adapt and innovate, to avoid losing even more of their members to the emerging churches. The strong Pentecostal presence may have also affected their doctrinal stance on a number of issues including polygamy.

Phillip Jenkins, in his 2007 book, The Next Christendom, the Coming of Global Christianity, shows how the weight of the global church has shifted to the Southern Hemisphere, and Africa, Latin America and South Asia are the new players in the future of Christianity. These churches also service the diaspora of the home nation abroad, who may provide the bulk of membership. This is true of El Shaddai Church from the Philippines and may soon become so for the Redeemed Christian Church of God from Nigeria.

The African Mega Churches

The largest Protestant churches in Egypt include the Evangelical Church of Egypt and the Episcopal Church in Jerusalem and the Middle East (Anglican Communion), Christian Brethren, Egyptian Baptist Convention and the Free Methodist Churches. Some Pentecostal churches with a presence in Egypt include the Assemblies of God Church of God of Prophecy, Pentecostal

Church of God and the Pentecostal Holiness Church.

The biggest and most influential of the new Pentecostal churches in Nigeria include the Redeemed Christian Church of God, Living Faith Church (Winners Chapel), Christ Embassy, and the DayStar Christian Centre. Others are the Lord's Chosen Charismatic Revival Ministries, Fountain of Life Church, Covenant Christian Centre, Latter Rain Assembly and House on The Rock. The list also includes the Redeemed Evangelical Mission, Deeper Life Gospel Church and Kingsway International Christian Centre (KICC). Other influential churches who may disagree theologically with those listed above include Mountain of Fire and Miracles Ministries (MFM) and the Synagogue Church of All Nations. Among the AIC churches who wear white garments and practice a more syncretic theology, one of the wealthiest is the Celestial Church of Christ.

In terms of the wealth of the top leadership of Nigeria's Pentecostal churches, Tim Cocks writing for Reuters reported that Forbes places the personal wealth of Bishop David Oyedepo (Winners Chapel) at $150 million, "Pastor Chris" Oyakhilome (Christ Embassy) at between $30 and $50 million, and TB Joshua, (Synagogue Church of All Nations) at $10 to $15 million. Surprisingly, he fails to add Pastor Enoch Adeboye (Redeemed Christian Church of God), who is rumoured to be one of the wealthiest men in Africa, if not in the world. Pastor Adeboye's office, naturally declines to comment on such matters...

The new Pentecostal churches preach healing through faith in Christ in all areas of life. Their Gospel is that faith in Jesus Christ (and obedience to the teaching of the Bible) can heal your spirit soul and body; and can also heal your bank account! The expansion of the new Pentecostal churches is not limited to Africa, several of them also run "mega-churches" in Europe and America. These churches are therefore major contributors to stemming the decline of church attendance in the Western nations. The growth of these churches in Africa and around the world seems set to continue. Another question is whether these mega-churches will use their "muscle" only for the growth of their own "kingdom" or for the benefit of the wider society…

Pentecostalism in Nigeria

As in many parts of Africa, Pentecostalism in Nigeria has been greatly influenced by the American versions of the movement, and has also followed the growing trends towards appointing Bishops, Apostles and Prophets etc. The emphasis on large "mega church" congregations, corporate level budgets and "superstar lifestyles" for the senior leadership. Unfortunately, the new Pentecostal churches have also not been without their own scandals, including messy divorces among leadership, financial misappropriation and sexual and other abuse of the vulnerable. These trends have left the new Pentecostals open to the same charges that they had levelled against the Roman Catholic and other historic denominations; of accumulating wealth and living life on a lavish scale. However the new Pentecostal churches are often highly entrepreneurial, not only starting churches from scratch without the benefit of historic buildings and administrative support, but also encouraging, incubating and birthing new businesses among their members. The new Pentecostal churches often make huge investments in their host communities.

It could also be argued that particularly in Africa where there is often a severe lack of infrastructure and services, these new churches provide a new sense of community, and can also make real contributions to the local economy. In the face of struggles with insecurity including militant Islamic terror, these churches have not just provided spiritual solace, but also practical relief to the internally displaced and other victims, as well as a degree of safety and strength in numbers.

The Third Wave

The first great wave of Christian evangelism after the New Testament times and the Early Church, came from Africa as the monastic movement born in Egypt, became the methodology of bringing Christianity to the far north of Europe. The next great wave was the sending out of Christian missionaries from Europe and America to different parts of the World. In modern times what has been the greatest comparable explosion of Christianity? No doubt the Pentecostal movement is the Third Wave of global Christianity, the greatest modern wave of revival and evangelism. That third wave effectively began on April 9, 1906, and would become known as the Azusa Street Revival in Los Angeles. It was led by William J. Seymour (an African American) and it is still continuing.

Modern Pentecostalism is impossible without Africa and the descendants of Africa. The music, preaching style and community focus of Pentecostalism are all typically "African".

Pentecostalism is not a new church, it's the latest revival in the church and it starts historically in a place called Azusa Street, with the sons and the daughters of Africa who had been forcibly taken out of Africa as a retribution for the contribution of Africa to the destiny of Christianity.

Those victims of the Trade in Enslaved Africans, were forcibly relocated into the Americas and the Caribbean but God raised up descendants of these sons and daughters of Africa with a new Pentecostal revival fire. Although there are missionaries and evangelists from all over the world, the greatest wave of Pentecostalism isn't coming from Europe; it's coming from Africa, Asia, and South America. The Pentecostal movements from Africa are sending their missionaries all over the world, including many to re-evangelise parts of Europe. Once again God calls on Africa to save the day. In these last days it is the destiny of Africa to help complete that work that was begun when the first evangelists spread out from Jerusalem, with the command to go to the entire world and make Disciples of every Nation.

In his 2007 book, "Spreading Fires: The Missionary Nature of Early Pentecostalism" Dr. Allan Anderson shows that the Pentecostal emphasis on the work of the Holy Spirit leads directly to the energy and commitment to evangelism and missions.

Our Future Destiny

A new people have emerged in Europe. They are a new African Diaspora. Many of them are now third and even fourth generation and now they are Europeans. You can't just keep calling them an Ethnic Minority. You can't keep calling them Caribbean. You can keep calling them Black African. We all should celebrate our heritage, but when I see them I see Europeans. I see British people. I see people who belong here, who have a home here, who have a destiny here. If you are one of them, it's about time you rose up and decide to methodically, take your place in that new British identity.

And it's about time you begin to teach your children (younger generation) to take their rightful place in the destiny of the nation where you live. Where is the Black British Prime Minister going to come from when you keep telling your children that they don't belong here? If you keep telling them they are strangers? After all you have suffered, all "your blood, your sweat, your tears"... After the "free labour" of your enslaved ancestors and the wealth of colonial empires has laid the foundations of the prosperity of the Western nations... After all the generations of the people who came over here as free men and women... and toiled to build nation, community and family... those who came before you and endured all kinds of things so that you could be here today.... "No blacks, no dogs, no Irish"... and all those many hundreds of thousands of Blacks and Asians who marched to war for the Kings and Queens of Europe... and bled and died for freedom and for this same Crown under which you live… *and you throw that all away and insult their memory by calling yourself a stranger in this land?* You are no stranger here! For the Earth is The Lord's… and the fullness thereof!

It is time for this "New African Diaspora" in Europe and the "Old African Diaspora" of the Americas and the Caribbean to join together, to come together at the table of the Lord and break the bread of Holy Communion that reconciles us. It is also time to be a viable part of practical solutions to the problems that affect the members of our churches and the wider community. The collective trauma of the people of Africa has allowed the forces of evil to feel they have a right to rule over us, even in our homes and over our children. For too long we have allowed ourselves to repeat the negative cycles that only entrench our ancient traumas more deeply into our collective psyche. We must repent, not just of the wrongs done to each other, but also for failing to be the generation that says *ENOUGH IS ENOUGH! THE CHANGE STARTS WITH US!*

Even the collectively traumatised can synergistically become the dynamic source for a global change of destiny. When Rev. Martin Luther King, Jr. and the allies of the Southern Christian Leadership Conference (SCLC) joined with the Dallas County Voters League (DCVL) and set out with the people to march from Selma to Montgomery, they did not know that they were stepping out to change the world. To coin a phrase, one small step by a few people can become a great leap from humankind. The American, Caribbean and European branches of the African Diaspora need to work together and with all people of goodwill like never before. For the first time we have the ability to stretch our hands across the globe as sons and daughters of Africa and sons and daughters of God through Christ. Out of Africa God has called His sons and His daughters into a time of destiny. This is not about "black liberation". It's about a global movement for physical, mental and spiritual liberation through the Gospel of Christ!

Until we complete our assignment, the Gospel will not be preached to the ends of the earth. In many parts of Europe and America now, as well as in other parts of the world there are families that have gone for generations without hearing the Gospel of Salvation. We must come together to play our part in this vital harvest. It's about the preparation for the coming of our Lord and our Saviour Jesus Christ, because without you the job can't be done. God has prepared Africans and Asians (and others from all over the world) as a people from ancient time for this time of destiny. As the Lord prepares and awaits the final ticking of the clock; the baton has fallen to us.

Final Reflections

In looking at Africa, Christianity and the Bible; our Global Destiny, we have briefly considered the origins of Africa's name and some of the African peoples, as well as their geographic distribution in ancient times; including some migrations in and out of Africa. We have looked at the ancient relationship between Africa and the story of the Bible, as well as some interactions between Africans and the people named in the Bible. Clearly, Africa was often important to the survival of the human ancestors of Christ, to the birth of Israel as a nation, and to the lives of several leaders in Israel including some of the Prophets. Far from being recent participants in the story of the Bible and Christianity, Africa and her children have been there from the beginning.

On reflection, we begin to understand why Africa has suffered the way that she has. It was not a curse of Ham that affected Africa as some have mistakenly taught. It was Canaan who was cursed prophetically because the Canaanites would desecrate Israel, the land which God called His own. God eventually had to eject them and He raised Israel in Africa to take their place. Contrary to those who have taught the "curse of Ham" hypothesis, Africa has been blessed to have always been part of the plan of God and the move of God; and as a consequence has been repeatedly traumatised, as a spiritual victim caught in that eternal battle... and like many trauma victims Africans have often come to tragically accept that trauma as their true identity... But the liberty that Jesus Christ proclaims, is far greater than the weight of any negative history

As much as we need to develop the physical infrastructure and administrative excellence of Africa, we also need to address the mental and spiritual components of our collective destiny. The churches cannot hide under a bushel of "spirituality" from the reality of their call to serve the people of the continent at every level of society. They cannot retreat into academic point-scoring that denies the transforming power of Christ. They cannot also abandon the precious gift of their natural African spirituality for the "good works" of the social Gospel. The Spirit needs a body that is prepared and willing to serve God and humanity, for the harvest is still plenteous and the labourers are still few. It is time for a new or renewed revival to change the identity of the churches, and their leaders of the churches. I believe that a new wave of revival is coming to the Pentecostal churches, especially those who have gradually become set in their routine ways, and are almost more religious than those they criticize. African Christians especially, need to understand their global destiny.

Relationships and destinies are both highly dependent on identity. This book is meant to help you gain new perspectives on the identity of Africa and her relationship with Christianity and the story of the Bible. It is time for the divisions of denomination and ethnicity in the church to be broken down, for black and white, ancient and modern churches to fulfil together the great prayer of Jesus Christ in John Chapter 17, that we may be one, as He and the Father are One.

Today is a day of destiny for somebody. I pray someone reading this is going to discover themselves in a totally different way. For up to now you may have been told so many things that have blinded your spiritual eyes to the truth of your divine destiny; that you have been called by God for this purpose; "out of Africa I have called you my son… I have called you my daughter". Will you take hold of the baton today? The generation that follows must be able to say that you and I did something about the destiny of our African people, and the destiny of the Gospel, which is the destiny of humanity and of all creation…

It is time for the churches across Africa to come together for the good of all of Africa and that includes discovering how they will relate to the real presence of Islam in Africa, including both the moderate and radical jihadist varieties.

Finally, we can see clearly the prophetic role of the descendants of Africa in these "last days of the Gospel", and in particular, we must see that the role of the new African Diaspora in Europe is linked with that of the African Diaspora in the Americas and the Caribbean. This challenges each of us to wake up, to understand our identity, and to pick up our destiny; and to leave a legacy of revival of the Gospel in our generation.

Selected Bibliography:

A Brief History Of Evangelisation in Africa, by Rev. Celestine A. OBI (Nigeria) http://www.afrikaworld.net/synod/obi.htm, (Tim Dowley, The Story of Christianity, 1981 pp.6,7)

Adogame, Afe; Gerloff, Roswith; and Hock, Klaus (2009) "Christianity in Africa and the African Diaspora: The Appropriation of a Scattered Heritage," African Diaspora Archaeology Newsletter: Vol. 12: Iss. 4, Article 1. Available at: http://scholarworks.umass.edu/adan/vol12/iss4/11

Anderson, A., 2007, Spreading Fires: The Missionary Nature of Early Pentecostalism, Orbis Books

Barbara W. Murck, Brian J. Skinner, Geology Today: Understanding Our Planet, Study Guide, Wiley, ISBN 978-0-471-32323-5

Benton, M.J. Vertebrate Palaeontology. Third edition (Oxford 2005), 25.

Brown, Thomas M Jr., Race and Interracial Marriage: A Biblical Survey and Perspective, http://www.creationism.org/csshs/v07n1p05.htm

Crosthwaite, T., The Gospel of Matthew -- for the Jews, from the article "Isaiah's Prophecy" by T. Crosthwaite, http://www.religioustolerance.org/crosthwaite01.ht m

Davidson, Basil, The Black Man's Burden: Africa and the Curse of the Nation State in Africa, James Currey, Sep 1992.

Elizabeth Isichei, A History of Christianity in Africa: From Antiquity to the Present (William B. Eerdmans Publishing Company, Grand Rapids, Michigan, 1995; Africa World Press, Inc., Lawrenceville, New Jersey, 1995)

Farmer, David H., Author, The Oxford Dictionary of Saints, Edition 5, Oxford University Press, 2004, Pages 28-29

Hale, Robert, W. Monasticism, Dyrness, William A. and Kärkkäinen Veli-Matti Et Al (Eds), Global Dictionary of Theology: A Resource for the Worldwide Church, IVP Academic 2008, Pages 574-575

Hemingway, Sean, and Colette Hemingway. "Africans in Ancient Greek Art". In Heilbrunn Timeline of Art History. New York: The Metropolitan Museum of Art, 2000–http://www.metmuseum.org/toah/hd/afrg/hd_afrg.htm (January 2008)

HIH Prince Ermias Sahle-Selassie Haile-Selassie, "The Origins of the Solomonic Dynasty and The Throne of David in Ethiopia", President of the Crown Council of Ethiopia, A Speech at the DuSable Museum of African-American History, June 29, 2014 (Used by Permission).

http://en.wikipedia.org

http://en.wikipedia.org/wiki/Semitic_people

http://ends.ng/boko-haram-big-oil-and-the-chad-connection/

http://jandyongenesis.blogspot.co.uk/2010/01/conversation-with-hausa-Moslem.html

http://jandyongenesis.blogspot.co.uk/2015/06/terah-means-priest.html

http://mymorningmeditations.com/2013/01/29/whatever-happened-to-the-mixed-multitude/

http://orthodoxwiki.org/The_Holy_Family_in_Egypt

http://st-takla.org/Coptic-church-1.html

http://theorthodoxchurch.info/blog/news/2011/07/an-ancient-syriac-orthodox-monastery-of-mor-augen-on-the-southern-slope-of-mount-izlo-in-turabdin-is-reopened/

http://www.afrikaworld.net/synod/obi.htm

http://www.afrikaworld.net/synod/obi.htm

http://www.alfagems.com

http://www.biblegateway.com

http://www.britannica.com/EBchecked/topic/26568
2/Saint-Hilarion

http://www.cfr.org/nigeria/boko-haram/p25739

http://www.icr.org/home/resources/resources_tract
s_whentheysawthestar/

http://www.jcrelations.net/The+Gospel+of+Mark+a
nd+Judaism.2208.0.html?L=3

http://www.newcriterion.com/articles.cfm/Stealing-
history-3624

http://www.opendoorsuk.org/persecution/worldwatc
h/egypt.php

http://www.rc.net/wcc/readings/lukeintr.htm

http://www.touregypt.net/holyfamily.htm#ixzz30e8y
GxzF

Isichei, Elizabeth, A History of Christianity in Africa:
From Antiquity to the Present, William B.
Eerdmans Publishing Company, Grand Rapids,
Michigan, 1995

Isleo, Bathsheba - A Truthful Account, Nov 2000, http://www.patriarchywebsite.com/bib-patriarchy/bathsheba-truthful-account.htm (accessed 08/04/2014)

J. Julius Scott, Jr. Gentiles and the Ministry of Jesus: Further Observations on Matt 10:5-6; 15:21-28, JETS 33/2 (June 1990) 161-169

Jenkins, P., 2007, The Next Christendom, the Coming of Global Christianity, Oxford University Press

Kamil, Jill, Coptic Egypt: History and Guide,The American University in Cairo Press, Cairo, Egypt, 1987

Kirk-Greene A., 1958, Adamawa Past and Present an Historical Approach to the Development of a Northern Cameroons Province, Oxford University Press

Lefkowitz, Mary, Not Out of Africa: How Afrocentrism Became an Excuse to Teach Myth as History, Basic Books, Reprint edition (1997)

Isichei, E., 1995, A History of Christianity In Africa From Antiquity to the Present, Society for Promoting Christian Knowledge (SPCK)

Matthew George Easton's Illustrated Bible Dictionary, Third Edition, published in 1897 by Thomas Nelson,

Oritsejafor, A., Nationalism and the Politics of National Security: The Christian and the Boko Haram Challenge, First Dr. Nnamdl Azikiwe Memorial Lecture on Nationalism and Igbo Leadership, Centre For Igbo Studies, University Of Nigeria Nsukka, Eminota Nigeria Limited #2 Amokwe Street, Uwani, Enugu, Nigeria

Rev. Celestine A. OBI (Nigeria), A Brief History of Evangelisation in Africa (Tim Dowley, The Story of Christianity, 1981 pp.6,7), http://www.afrikaworld.net/synod/obi.htm

S.E. Bird, S., & Ottanelli, F., 2014, The Asaba Massacre and the Nigerian Civil War: Reclaiming Hidden History, Journal of Genocide Research, 16:2-3, 379-399.

Schaff, Philip and Wace, Henry (Eds), Vol. 4: ST. ATHANASIUS Selected Works and Letters - Nicene & Post-Nicene Fathers, Series II (The Early Church Fathers), Wm. B. Eerdmans, 1953

The Establishment Of The Ethiopian Church, By Professor Sergew Habele Selassie, http://www.ethiopianorthodox.org/english/ethiopian /prechristian.html

The Holy Bible, New King James Version , Thomas Nelson, Inc. 1982

Ware, T., The Orthodox Church, Harmondsworth: Penguin, 1964

Orr, J., Gen Ed, 1915, Vol1, The International Standard Bible Encyclopaedia, The Howard-Severance Company

Yong, A., (Ed), Estrelda Y. Alexander, E., (Ed), 2012, Afro-Pentecostalism: Black Pentecostal and Charismatic Christianity in History and Culture, NYU Press

Zeeya Merali, Brian J. Skinner, Visualizing Earth Science, Wiley, ISBN 978-0-470-41847-5